The Magic Flute

MASTERWORKS
OF OPERA

General Editor: Charles Osborne

To Bryan Corrie,
with whom I have experienced
enjoyed and discussed
so much Mozart.

PETER GAMMOND

The Magic Flute

A GUIDE TO THE OPERA

FOREWORD BY
BENJAMIN LUXON

BARRIE & JENKINS

Designed and produced by Breslich & Foss, London

© Breslich & Foss 1979

First published in 1979 by Barrie & Jenkins
An imprint of the Hutchinson Publishing Group
3 Fitzroy Square, London W1P 6JD

Design: Craig Dodd
Picture Research: Philippa Lewis

Filmset and printed in Great Britain by
BAS Printers Limited, Over Wallop, Hampshire

ISBN 0 214 20681 5

Contents

Foreword by Benjamin Luxon

My first acquaintance with *The Magic Flute* was at about the age of nine. My father was an amateur bass singer of some renown, and I was 'treading the boards' as a boy soprano in a Cornwall that was alive with singing and concert making. My father's favourite song was 'Isis and Osiris'. It seemed to inspire the very best in his voice and was always requested by concert organizers and audiences. Amongst a musical diet of Victorian and Edwardian songs and ballads, interlaced with music from Handel's oratorios, Mozart's wonderful aria stood out for me as a very different musical entity. My curiosity being aroused, I read through the words hoping to find a story line I had missed, but found only references to wisdom and eternal life. Still I remember distinctly that my father's singing and stature seemed to grow in dignity and warmth when performing this aria. With no musical qualifications other than an instinct for singing and love of music, neither of us was aware of the opera from which it originated, but the seed had been sown.

Some twelve years later as a student teacher in London, I saw *The Magic Flute* at last. I couldn't pretend to understand what was happening, but there was something about the overall effect of the music, the sequence of events and number of characters involved that seemed to awaken in me some deep response and the knowledge that this opera was unique. In subsequent years I saw enough of *The Magic Flute* to begin to know its complicated plot, develop sympathies with its characters and intensify my deep love of its music.

With the change from teaching music to singing, I became totally immersed in the world of music and realized that with my type of voice I would be able to sing the role of Papageno in my favourite Mozart opera. In spite of this I was not to sing the role until I was forty-one. By this time I had sung Guglielmo, Count Almaviva, and Don Giovanni, and through study and particularly through performance, had come to some understanding of Mozart's extraordinary genius. Therefore, by the time I came to portray the role, my instinctive feelings had germinated into a very clear personal view of the world of allegory and symbolism that is *The Magic Flute*.

Papageno is a wonderful creation for the actor-singer. He can be played in many ways: as a pure comic, as the confidante of his audience, as the naïve flesh-and-blood child of nature, the down-to-earth peasant worker, the quick Peter Pan-like opportunist. Whichever way he is played, however, the simplicity and warmth of his music, combined with his vulnerability in a world of bewildering encounters and events, makes him irresistible. There is not a person in the audience who cannot identify with some aspect of him—either his fear, amazement, excitement, frustration, cheekiness, bluster, sadness or happiness—and understand and love him. He is 'everyman' in embryo. With his simple needs in a world beyond his control, Papageno symbolizes what is so often the reality of life. With their pure love and courage, Tamino and Pamina symbolize man's possibility of fulfilling his highest potential in life.

In playing Papageno, I set myself certain basic tasks: firstly, to make him as warm and open as possible; secondly, to try always to bear in my mind that as far as we know he has never seen another human being (apart from the three ladies) and never a house or building (apart from his straw hut); and finally, with this as his basic 'character', to react instinctively to whatever is happening.

Looking back, I can now understand the 'pull' this music had for my father. Mozart and Schikaneder have created for us an optimistic and magical allegory of life itself, the music of which is the voice that speaks to our innermost being.

The Magic Flute

OPERA IN TWO ACTS BY
WOLFGANG AMADEUS MOZART

Background to the Opera

There are few, if any, major operas now in the regular repertoire that have aroused as much speculation or controversy as *Die Zauberflöte*, or *The Magic Flute*. Nearly everyone who writes about the opera feels impelled to start with some apologia on the lines of the comments written by Stephen Williams in his *Come to the Opera* first published in 1948: '*The Magic Flute* is no doubt the most fantastic mixture of the sublime and the ridiculous ever put on the stage. We fidget in our seats as one grotesque absurdity succeeds another; and then—something happens; one of these preposterous puppets begins to sing—is, as it were, illumined by song, dissolved into music; and what was before mere pantomime trickery becomes ageless and timeless magic, the very revelation of godhead.' Earlier, in 1913, Edward J. Dent in his classic book *Mozart's Operas*, said that it was possible to consider the libretto as being 'one of the most absurd specimens of that form of literature in which absurdity is regarded as a matter of course'. Ernest Newman, like most writers since, found 'its origins wrapped in mystery'. Recent commentators are more at home in a world where musical and artistic incomprehensibility has become commonplace. The combination of a deep search for religious and philosophic truth and pantomime tomfoolery perhaps worries us less today than it did in the nineteenth century when *The Magic Flute* was rarely staged and Mozart was not so wholeheartedly accepted as a major composer. Today our admiration for his music makes its hybrid story seem less important, but there is still a great fascination in the background of freemasonry which has been examined with almost excessive zeal in Jacques Chailley's *The Magic Flute, Masonic Opera* (1972).

With so much having been said on the subject it is almost impossible to add anything new. Perhaps, as in so many cases in musical history, it would now be a good thing to say less and listen more. *The Magic Flute* is accepted as one of the world's

ABOVE: *Mozart as a teen-ager with his sister and father, seated by a portrait of his mother*

greatest operas, though it is still difficult to stage it with conviction. But today we are in the fortunate position of being able to listen to half-a-dozen excellent versions of it on the gramophone where the music can be enjoyed with less distraction. It should certainly be our aim to enjoy it in an unbiased and uncomplicated frame of mind; at the same time appreciating the various historical and personal elements that led to its creation.

Firstly, we should briefly consider Mozart himself and the kind of composer that he was. This, to start with, is a difficult assessment to make, as comparatively little is known about his creative activities, his working method and what inspired him. His own comments, mainly to be found in his letters, are often unhelpful in being essentially practical and rarely self-revealing.

They are mainly either a terse comment to the effect that for some imminent concert he has composed two or three new pieces (for which he has inevitably been under-paid or not paid at all); or they are the eminently down-to-earth comments of a working musician. With specific reference to opera, he suggests in a letter to his father in 1777 that it would be ideal if he could draw up a contract with an influential nobleman to compose four German operas every year and be allowed a benefit performance of each. His main concern is clearly that such an effort would bring in 500 gulden a year. His most revealing comments are on the lines of 'I like an aria to fit a singer as perfectly as a well-made suit of clothes' or 'if only that confounded French tongue was not so detestable for music—it really is hopeless, even German is divine by comparison'.

Faced with the remarkable fluency of his genius, those who find the writing of music a mystery, or even those who struggle over a small task of orchestration for the local operatic society, sometimes find it difficult to comprehend that someone like Mozart was writing music as naturally as most of us write a letter—possibly with greater ease. He was already composing when he was five. In a comparatively short life he wrote some seven or eight hundred works including twenty completed operas. As *The Magic Flute* was one of the main tasks occupying Mozart's last year on earth, we inevitably think of it as a work of his maturity. *His* maturity certainly; but it will give us a better sense of the work's stature, its weaknesses as well as its greatness, if we remember that Mozart was only in his thirty-fifth year when he wrote it, which is not a great age in terms of maturity and experience. Verdi had not even started on his great operatic period at thirty-five, and *Rigoletto* was still three years ahead of him. Wagner had written *Rienzi* and *The Flying Dutchman*, but the bulk of his achievement was still to come. In lighter opera terms, the Gilbert and Sullivan partnership had just begun. Haydn at the same age had got to around No. 35 in his symphonic output, while Brahms was a venerable forty when he wrote his first symphony.

In the year of his death, sick and frail, Mozart wrote his last Piano Concerto, the Clarinet Concerto, numerous dances, a string quintet, several arias and the motet '*Ave verum corpus*', several miscellaneous instrumental and vocal works, two operas—*La Clemenza di Tito* and *The Magic Flute*—and most of

13

the famous *Requiem*. This inevitably leads us to surmise as to how much pre-consideration he needed to give to such sublime works—the sort of philosophical and analytical consideration that is implied in most critical comment; or how much of it was a natural almost unconsidered flow. There is no indication that Mozart was an intellectual in outlook and his academic education was negligible. He was very much a practical musician, a performer as well as a composer, and that fact should surely always be kept in mind.

OPPOSITE: *An engraving showing Mozart at the keyboard* c. *1785*

To accept him as a 'working musician' is not simply to regard him as a musical machine. Certainly he was a machine in many respects; a sort of magical computer or robot in modern terms. His friend and pupil Attwood has told us how Mozart would leave the company at the end of a meal, politely excusing himself on the grounds of some work to be done, to return an hour or so later in satisfied good spirits having conceived and scored a substantial work. The completed score would be the finished product, completely notated and marked for performance with rarely a note or an accent needing to be altered. He would often continue to work while holding a conversation. It seems that he only put pen to paper when the conception of the composition was complete in his mind. His early biographer Otto Jahn coined the phrase 'unusual power of detachment' to describe Mozart's working method. We come to the end of speculation by inevitably dragging in the word 'inspiration'. It was not so much that he was a composing machine but that he could clear his mind of all other considerations and, having decided what was the best way to tackle the problem in hand, was able to switch on the current of inspiration, which most creators tap intermittently or without complete control of the when and wherefore, more or less at will.

This conception gives us a clear, if still ultimately inexplicable, view of how Mozart could turn out works as required and how he could tackle a libretto like *The Magic Flute* and in a remarkably short time produce an inspired score that transformed an often pedestrian libretto into a musical masterpiece. His method was in direct contrast to Beethoven's, for instance, who, we know from his sketchbooks and frequently altered scores, continually changed and refined his ideas while he was writing. The end result is the same; but Mozart thought first and wrote afterwards. The nature of the music that Mozart

15

produced is, however, still an enigma. While all the facts of his life persuade us that Mozart was not in any way a mystic there is still a truly mystical quality about his writing. Two valid comparisons might be made with the music of Haydn and Schubert. Without for a moment devaluing Haydn's music, which has visibly grown in stature over recent years as it has been thoroughly rediscovered, is it not the music of a craftsman who found his inspiration during the actual assembling of the notes? Compared to Mozart's music Haydn's is frequently less inspired but carried surely along by his skills and ingenuity. Now that we know his operas more thoroughly can we honestly say, in spite of our admiration for their craft and many delights, that any one of them can come within reach of *Figaro*. Schubert was a musical lyricist, delighting in the capture of a felicitous idea but also depending very much, in his vocal writing, on the inspiration the words offered. He failed to write a great opera because he never came across an inspired libretto. What would these great composers have produced when faced with the 'farrago of ideas' that Mozart was presented with in *The Magic Flute*? Beethoven would never have attempted it; Haydn would have produced something worthy and polished; Schubert would have tried, perhaps managed a couple of inspired arias and have left the project unfinished. Mozart simply accepted it as he might have accepted an awkward position on the billiard table, found the ideal solution to the problem and executed it perfectly.

An excellent analysis of Mozart's musical qualities is to be found in Arthur Hutching's book *Mozart: The Man—The Musician* which goes into all the elements that have been briefly examined above. Again the conclusion reached is that, while Mozart was not a mystic in character, his music, once it has passed the apprentice stage of his boyhood, has an unbroken strain of mysticism in it. There is a rightness and an unfailing ability to produce something out of the ordinary in everything he wrote. As far as our eventual assessment of *The Magic Flute* goes, we must always accept that Mozart never thought consciously of all the various layers of meaning that commentators later imposed on it; his mental processes were incredibly condensed and intense so that he produced instinctively what others might perhaps produce by prolonged labour and thought.

By the time he came to write his first dramatic piece *Die Schuldigkeit des ersten Gebotes* (The Obligation of the First and Foremost Commandment) early in 1767 at the age of eleven, he was a seasoned performer, composer and traveller and had visited and played in Vienna, Paris and London and many other towns en route. Much of his already assured vocal technique he learned from Johann Christian Bach who, as the Queen's Music Master, had been officially concerned with Mozart's appearance at Court during his fifteen-month stay in England during 1764 and 1765, and who had become a close friend and mentor of the young Mozart. During his stay in London and Tunbridge Wells Mozart often heard and was duly influenced by Bach's music whose style and technique are clearly reflected in Mozart's early works. In the operatic field Bach's elegant writing, pure melodies and leanings toward what was later to be known as *bel canto*—a concern with beauty of phrase and technique rather than dramatic substance—had their early effect on Mozart's own vocal writing. It was elegant rather than profound music but it was forward-looking in its techniques. During the season of 1764–5 Bach's operas were being produced at the King's Theatre; pastiches like *Berenice*, and his *Adriano in Siria* were

ABOVE: *Design for The Magic Flute by Oskar Laske (left) and costume design for Papageno by Stürmer for the 1816 Berlin production*

played there during January 1765. The Mozarts went to the theatre and were excited, as all London was, by the magical voice of the renowned castrato Giovanni Manzuoli who was supported by an excellent cast of Italian singers. Such an aria as '*Son sventurato, ma pure o stelle*' which Mazuelo sang in *Adriano* has a strong foretaste of Mozart in it.

The Mozarts also made contact with Thomas Arne whose *Arterxerxes* had been a great success at Covent Garden in 1763 and who wrote an opera *L'Olimpiade* for the King's Theatre season of 1765. His English 'vulgarity' was generally considered inferior to Bach's Germanic elegance and it has never been suggested that Mozart learned much from Arne. Nevertheless this operatic experience added to his qualifications, so it was not surprising that the Archbishop of Salzburg had every confidence in him when he asked him to compose the music for the first part of a sacred singspiel *Die Schuldigkeit des ersten Gebotes* to the text 'And thou shalt love the Lord thy God with all thy heart, and with all thy soul, and with all thy mind, and with all thy strength'. The other two parts were supplied by Salzburg's leading composers, Johann Michael Haydn (younger brother of Joseph Haydn) and Anton Cajetan Adlgasser, Concertmaster and Chamber Composer–Organist respectively to His Serene Highness. The librettist was simply credited as J. A. W. and was probably a Salzburg merchant Herr Weiser, although others have been credited. Mozart supplied a Sinfonia (Overture) and eight vocal items written with his usual facility and speed and reportedly unaided. He received, as his reward, a gold medal of twelve ducats. The music is competent and generally charming, and Mozart thought enough of one gentle allegro aria for the tenor part of the Spirit of Christianity '*Manches Übel will zuweilen*' to use it again in his first full-scale opera *La finta semplice (The Pretended Simpleton)*.

Another commission followed immediately; to write the music for a short opera (or musical intermezzo) *Apollo et Hyacinthus* for the entertainment given by the University students of Salzburg at the end of each scholastic term. The text was by the Professor of Syntax, Father Rufinius Widl, and the music that Mozart provided pleased everyone who heard it. While some commentators like Edward J. Dent and Alfred Einstein have dismissed these early Mozart efforts as not worth hearing and mere imitations of Bach, they are essential and

19.

18.
Tamino mit der Zauberflöte.
Tamino avec la flûte enchantée.

17.

16.
Die Sclaven.
Les Esclaves.

14.
Pamina.

13.
Sarastro.

12.
Die Königin der Nacht.
La Reine de la Nuit.

11.

9.
Die Priester.
Les Prêtres.

8.
Die Knaben.
Les Garçons.

7.
Die Damen.
Les Dames.

6.

4.
Papagena.

3.
Papageno.

2.
Der schwarze Monostatos.
Le noir Monostatos.

1.
Die Schlange.
Le serpent.

remarkable steps in a sure and forward-moving operatic development. The Mozartian traits are clearly there in *Apollo et Hyacinthus*; in an aria for Zephyrus, '*En! duos conspicis*', and especially in an attractive duet, '*Natus cadit, atque Deus*', sung by the characters Oebalus and Melia.

Even so accomplished a child as Mozart seems to have been unduly hustled into his first full length operatic work, an *opera buffa* in three acts, *La finta semplice*, to a libretto by the court poet Marco Coltellini. At this time the Mozarts were in Vienna and it was the Emperor Joseph II who suggested that Mozart should write an opera and who helped to coerce a somewhat reluctant manager Giuseppe Affligio to draw up a contract with a promised fee of one hundred ducats. Mozart, as ever eager and ready to oblige, immediately set to work. The singers liked what they saw and heard of the music but Affligio procrastinated in every possible way, eventually went bankrupt and left Vienna without the opera being produced.

Certain malicious persons spread rumours at the time that the score was not written by the young Mozart but by his father Leopold. Leopold was highly indignant and organized a demonstration at which Mozart spontaneously set to music any text that anyone cared to present to him. This quietened the critics but a theatrical production of *La finta semplice* still failed to materialize and the Mozarts found themselves penniless in Vienna. The Archbishop of Salzburg took pity on them and organized a concert performance in his palace on May 1, 1769. After that it was forgotten until the Mozart revival of recent years. The importance of the opera is simply that it shows the real beginnings of the Mozart operatic style, firmly based on Italian traditions. If one cares to find pre-echoes, Polidoro's aria, No. 7 in the score, certainly has a vague hint of Papageno's '*bouche-fermée*' aria in *The Magic Flute*. As this was itself mainly lifted from his earlier *Die Schuldigkeit* one begins to get some notion of the improvisatory nature of much operatic writing of the time. In Giacinta's aria (No. 24) there is a thematic resemblance to the first number in *The Magic Flute*, which is not an indication of any later lack of ideas but simply an interesting example of a composer already settling into a musical style inevitably made up of phrases and harmonies that have become as natural as turns of speech. *La finta semplice* is a naïve work but

OPPOSITE: *Two different stage designs: Covent Garden production of 1947, set by Oliver Messel* (above); *1967 Metropolitan Opera production, the final scene, set by Chagall* (below)

it is already full of the typical Mozartian charm and vivacity, of gems in an imperfect setting.

With *Bastien und Bastienne* we come to a work that could with greater confidence be described as a minor masterpiece and at least the seed of a style that would end up as the luxuriant growth of his later operas. It was commissioned by Anton Mesmer, the later famous inventor of mesmerism and a prominent Freemason, and set to a German translation of a popular French comedy already used for an opera by Johann Adam Hiller. Its first performance was given privately in Mesmer's garden in Vienna. A performance in Salzburg was planned but did not materialize and it was not revived until the 1890s. It was not actually heard in Salzburg until 1928. It is essentially a miniature opera with a cast of three and a mini-overture whose opening theme curiously anticipates the opening of Beethoven's *Eroica* symphony some thirty-five years later, though there is absolutely no evidence of Beethoven having any acquaintance with the opera. Simply a case of great minds thinking alike, only remarkable because one of the great minds was that of a twelve-year-old boy. Important to our distant preview of *The Magic Flute* is the fact that this is a setting of German rather than Italian words with the perceptible difference in musical phrasing that this enforces. Preparatory work for *The Magic Flute* is to be found in the C-minor aria (No. 10) where Mozart sets an entirely frivolous text to serious and portentous music leading to a dialogue in which Colas promises that Bastien shall see his sweetheart and talk to her if he shows more responsibility toward his birthright of happiness. This certainly has more than a hint of Sarastro's demands upon Tamino. *Bastien und Bastienne* is an important harbinger of the later German operas. It emphasizes, more than anything, Mozart's acute sensitivity to words—already noted in a quotation from one of his letters.

Through the influence of Count Firmian, the governor of Lombardy, Mozart was now commissioned to write an opera for Milan. This was *Mitridate, Re di Ponto* (*Mithridates, King of Pontus*) which he wrote in 1770 and which was performed on December 26. It was a clear imitation of the prevalent Italian style with plenty of opportunity for vocal virtuosity and led to a further commission for *Ascanio in Alba*, produced in October 1771, a piece of little dramatic significance, a mixture of ballet

ABOVE AND OPPOSITE: *Costume and set designs from the 1816 Berlin production display the Egyptian and masonic themes of Mozart's opera.*

and cantata, more a masque than an opera.

Il Sogno di Scipione (*Scipio's Dream*) that followed was, like the earlier *Die Schuldigkeit*, written for an episcopal occasion, this time to celebrate the enthronement of the new Archibishop of Salzburg, Count Colloredo. It was a special piece privately performed and early Mozart commentators usually dismiss it in a sentence or so; but, as with anything written by Mozart it is worthy of attention and rediscovery. Count Firmian sub-sequently commissioned another opera from Mozart for the 1772–3 Milan season. Now a mature seventeen, he treated the creation of *Lucio Silla* in a thoroughly business-like manner. One interesting point in connection with the piece is that the libretto was supplied by Giovanni de Gamerra who later was to make the standard Italian translation of *The Magic Flute*—in which language it was to become known to many London opera-goers in the nineteenth century. It is not easy to get excited about the work as a drama, but as ever it contains much fine music written in a fashionable vein, yet often showing Mozart's individual dramatic abilities. It was a trial run for an *opera seria* soon to be consummated in *Idomeneo*.

At this point it is important to look at some incidental music that he wrote for a play by Tobias Philipp von Gebler in 1773, *Thamos, König in Ägypten* (*Thamos, King of Egypt*). The play was first produced in Vienna in April 1774 and in Salzburg in 1777 (without Mozart's music); and five years later Mozart revised his original score, re-writing several choruses and adding various sections (the version now generally heard on record) for a touring Salzburg company. They also used the music in connection with another play. This was Mozart's first important contact with the masonic ideals that he was to promote so wholeheartedly in *The Magic Flute*. Gebler had approached several composers, including Gluck, who were Freemasons like himself, before he rejected a score by Johann Tobias Sattler and finally entrusted the task to Mozart; on what basis we cannot be certain, but possibly on the recommendation of other Masons who saw in the serious-minded boy a potential recruit to their circle. As early as 1767, when Mozart had been cured of smallpox by Dr Joseph Wolfe of Olmutz, he had sent, as a token of gratitude, an arietta '*An die Freude*' which was set to a masonic text possibly supplied by the parish priest at Olmutz. Around the same period, as already noted, he had written *Bastien und Bastienne* for the prominent Freemason Dr Anton Mesmer who was later, in 1783, to found a masonic society in Paris, the '*Ordre de l'Harmonie universelle*' for the purpose of purifying initiates through mesmerism. Other earlier pieces by Mozart that have been accorded masonic significance through association were his setting of the penitential psalm '*De profundis clamavi*' in 1771 and the song '*O heiliges Band der Freundschaft*' in 1772, neither of which were directly intended as masonic pieces but were co-opted into the masonic repertoire for their espousement of the ideals of co-fraternity, the latter being adapted from its original soprano range to tenor.

If Mozart was by no means committed to these ideals in 1773 there is little question that a person of his sensibility must have absorbed much of the message of *Thamos* and certainly responded to its mystical message; even if it was all embedded in what one commentator has called 'a mish-mash of Masonry and Egyptology'. A full account of the plot can be found in

Charles Osborne's *The Complete Operas of Mozart*. The final music for *Thamos* consists of three choruses and five entr'actes. The first chorus '*Schon weichet dir, Sonne*' greets the rising sun. Its solemn maestoso grandeur is quite unlike anything Mozart had so far incorporated in any of his operas and we can hardly dissociate it from the similar chorus by Sarastro and his followers in the final scenes of *The Magic Flute*. There is no question that it has a deep devotional quality that we rarely find even in Mozart's other church music which is mainly couched in more joyful baroque terms. If Mozart was not, at this point, in any way committed to masonry, he was certainly already aware of its spirit and meaning—and it obviously meant much to him. The final lines of Act One have sentiments that we will hear again in the ordeal scenes of *The Magic Flute*, 'Mirza is a woman and does not tremble. You are a Man. Conquer or die!', to which Mozart responds, as in the overture to *The Magic Flute*, with three solemn chords, probably requested by Gebler. The next chorus '*Gottheit über alle mächtig*' is again a chorus of thanksgiving by the priests and handmaidens of the sun and again the pre-echoes of *The Magic Flute* are unmistakable. In the final chorus '*Ihr Kinder des Staubes*' a high priest tells the people to fear the wrath of God, a clear model for Sarastro's similar warnings, followed by a joyful chorus of thanksgiving. The music, as so often happens, was far superior to the drama which was soon forgotten. Mozart obviously thought it one of his finest early achievements and was still hoping to have the play revived for the sake of the music in 1783, as he mentions in a letter to his father. The entr'actes were forgotten for nearly a century, but the choruses, given latin texts, were taken over by the church and were regarded as important examples of Mozart's religious music, a somewhat ironic situation. That *Thamos* was still in Mozart's mind when he wrote *The Magic Flute* is beyond doubt and a study of the opera should certainly be prefaced by a hearing of this splendid and impressive music, now easily available on record.

Between the early and later productions of *Thamos*, Mozart was engaged on a further conventional *opera buffa* in the Italian manner, *La finta giardiniera* (*The Pretended Garden-Girl*) which had three very well-received performances in Munich in 1775. It remained a popular work, was revived in a German translation as *Die Gärtnerin aus Liebe* in 1780 by many travelling companies, and was regularly in the repertoire until around 1797. It was the best opera that Mozart had yet written, in spite of a feeble libretto, a foretaste of his mastery of the Italian comic opera and the future perfection of *Figaro*. *Il re pastore* (*The Shepherd King*), a '*dramma per musica*', was written for the Salzburg court in 1775 and had one or two delightful arias. Aminta's aria '*L'amèro*', with violin obbligato, achieved lasting popularity, but after one or two performances the opera was forgotten and not revived until 1906 when it was performed in Munich and Salzburg on the 150th anniversary of Mozart's birth.

The surprising gap of five years between *Il re pastore* and Mozart's next commissioned opera *Idomeneo* was only filled in dramatic terms by the revival of *Thamos* and an incomplete German singspiel *Zaide* which might have been intended for the same company or perhaps for the touring company of Emanuel Schikaneder, by now a friend of the family who regularly visited Salzburg during this period. The surviving music is of great interest but is mainly of a static nature. In 1777, before Mozart left Salzburg for his long tour of Mannheim, Paris and other places in the Autumn, he composed a gradual *ad festum* to the Virgin Mary '*Sancta Maria, mater Dei*', a work, for four-voiced chorus and strings with organ bass, of great simplicity and beauty. It was yet another piece that was to find itself adopted by the masonic brotherhood; a demonstration of the movement's lack of bias in matters of religious affiliation; a catholicism of thought that was rarely reciprocated by the established churches.

The five-year interval now seems of the utmost significance. We can see it as a time when Mozart was not only re-charging his creative batteries, even if involuntarily, but was throwing off the muddling influences of Italian opera and moving toward his own truly individual creations in the *genre*. Certainly most of the works that come after, with one or two minor exceptions, are major masterpieces and include *Idomeneo*, *The Seraglio*, *The Marriage of Figaro*, *Don Giovanni*, *Così fan tutte* and *The Magic Flute*—what a magical list of names! While in Mannheim, Mozart had been promised by the Elector that a commission for a new opera was a certainty. But it was not until 1780 that he received the order for a new work for the Munich carnival season of 1780–1. Mozart had much wanted to write an opera in German, a growing pre-occupation in the face of the Italian domination, but the new one was wanted in Italian and, of course, Mozart complied. As a compromise Mozart suggested to his librettist, Giovanni Battista Varesco, an opera in the French manner, a unified drama with plenty of ensemble work. He began to write *Idomeneo* early in October 1780, and it was finished and performed by January 29, 1781, two days after his twenty-fifth birthday. It was well received and has never lacked performances since.

The hints of *The Magic Flute* are naturally stronger than ever in this mature work, his supreme *opera seria*, though the opera is of a totally different nature, a lead toward the serious dramatic opera that he would certainly have written had he lived longer, and which would probably have provided an even closer link with *Fidelio* and the Wagnerian epics. For many *Idomeneo* lacks the essential lightness and humour of the Mozart they love. Henceforth true seriousness was to come intermingled with comedy; an accomplishment which, as in *The Magic Flute*, might be considered Mozart's greatest dramatic innovation.

With *The Seraglio* he created his first important German opera with the encouragement and support of the Austrian Emperor Joseph II who saw no reason why the German stage should be dominated by Italians and created a National Singspiel theatre. Mozart eyed this new development hopefully. Eventually the request came and he turned to Gottlieb Stephanie 'the younger' for a libretto adapted from a 1780 work by Christoph Friedrich Bretzner which had already been used several times as an opera. It was written in an oriental vein so popular in the theatre of the time though, in effect, the so-called Turkish elements, here as elsewhere in Mozart's music, really amount to nothing more than a little extra percussion. At last Mozart was writing for a well-trained cast and specific singers whom he knew and admired. He received the first draft of the libretto in July 1781 and it was first produced on July 16, 1782 in the Burgtheater. It had a noisy reception and the Emperor thought that it had too many notes. Thereafter it was frequently played in Vienna and remained Mozart's most popular opera in his lifetime. It was not heard in England until 1827. It was his best comic opera up to that time. Neither it nor *Idomeneo* was particularly related to *The Magic Flute*, except in being obviously by the same composer. Each of his major operas from now on seemed to be directed on an interestingly different tack.

27

RIGHT: *Josef Lange
(1751–1831), painter
and actor at the Court
Theatre in Vienna and
his wife Aloysia whose
sister married Mozart*

RIGHT: *Josef Lange (1751–1831), painter and actor at the Court Theatre in Vienna and his wife Aloysia whose sister married Mozart*

If these two masterpieces were expected to establish Mozart as a leading opera composer there was some disappointment in this respect. It was another four years before he was commissioned again. Soon after *The Seraglio* he had married Constanze Weber and now had to labour as a responsible married man, giving up much valuable time to teaching but still managing, through poor direction of his affairs, to remain on the poverty line. His insistence that the future lay in German opera was once more contradicted when, again with the assistance of Giovanni Battista Varesco, he wrote *L'Oca del Cairo* (*The Goose of Cairo*). By this time he had met Lorenzo da Ponte who had expressed a desire to work with him and from whom Mozart would have liked to have had a new and original

script. But Da Ponte was involved with Salieri and for the moment Varesco had to do. It was not a happy interlude. Mozart got the first act more or less completed and then gave up. It was the silliest story he had ever been presented with and the music was not nearly as good as that of *The Seraglio*. The next opera *Lo Sposo Deluso* (*The Outwitted Bridegroom*) is something of a mystery. The uncredited libretto is often presumed to be by Lorenzo da Ponte but the truth is not certain. If it was, it was an inauspicious start to a great partnership because Mozart managed only an overture and four songs before he abandoned it. There was a first-rate cast waiting; some of whom were later in *Figaro*. The music was masterly in the fragments that were achieved, so why did it get no further? And was the odd libretto

really by Da Ponte? If it was, then it may have been an early piece that he gave Mozart to try his hand on. Mozart obviously wished for better.

By 1786 the real collaboration with Da Ponte had begun and Mozart was already at work on *The Marriage of Figaro*. He put it aside for a while to obey a royal command from Emperor Joseph II for a piece for an Imperial occasion. Gottlieb Stephanie was similarly commanded to supply the text. The resulting *Der Schauspieldirektor (The Impresario)* is a pleasant well-turned work with a surprisingly grandiose overture for a one-act comedy. But there were only four other musical items of not great significance in an overlong text full of topical allusions. Nobody has been completely decided how best to produce it ever since, although there have been numerous attempts.

To speak at all of the three great masterpieces *The Marriage of Figaro*, *Don Giovanni* and *Così fan tutte* which Mozart wrote to texts by Da Ponte is a temptation to speak at length. In this brief study directed toward *The Magic Flute* we can only consider where each lay in relation to this opera. *The Marriage of Figaro* (1786) is perhaps the greatest comic opera the world has had, certainly the most shapely and consistently melodic. Based on the immortal play by Beaumarchais (the sequel to *The Barber of Seville*), it was ideally adapted by Da Ponte at Mozart's suggestion. It is a long and immensely detailed opera, but it never seems anything but compact and well-balanced. In it Mozart came to write the most sparkling and light-hearted of melodies with a classical perfection of form; and to balance these with charmingly serious arias of love and sorrow. He was at last writing music for believable characters. All these things were to be a great asset when it came to making something out of *The Magic Flute*. *Don Giovanni* (1787) variously described as a *dramma giocoso* or an *opera buffa* took the inner contrasts a good step or two further. It is a romantic and melodramatic masterpiece on the one hand and yet it is full of light comedy and vivacious music. Its characters are more deeply portrayed and the music is stronger than in *Figaro* even if it has not got the same architectural perfection. It is an opera far ahead of its time and not so far removed from what Verdi was doing in his prime *Rigoletto* period. *Così fan tutte* (1790) came at a time when Mozart was able to spend time on the score and to prod his collaborator

OPPOSITE: *Mozart's wife Constanze. A painting made in 1802 by Hans Hansen and probably commissioned by her second husband*

31

into a well-finished and polished libretto; in fact the libretto is its great strength, well developed, logically moving, full of fascinating detail. It is a tidy, classical opera, and, in many ways, the score is Mozart's best, even if it has not the same personality as *Figaro* and *Giovanni* or the same ration of 'hit' songs. While it will never be as popular as the others, wise men agree that it is unsurpassed.

In turning back to the *dramma seria per musica* of *La Clemenza di Tito* (*The Clemency of Titus*) Mozart has been considered by some to have lost his way. Perhaps, in his illness and worry he could not be expected to care very much about an opera demanded for the festivities of 1791 when Leopold II was to be crowned King of Bohemia. Leopold had pointedly ignored Mozart in favour of lesser musicians on every possible occasion. The gloomy story by Pietro Metastasio is heavy going, the arias are short and the orchestration is not particularly detailed. Though there is every sign that Mozart wrote an opera without much sense of commitment, the Mozartian enthusiast will rightly insist that anything by Mozart is worth hearing. Recent revivals, as at Covent Garden in 1975, and a good modern recording have restored interest in the work but it is unlikely that it will ever become a favourite.

The creation of *The Magic Flute*, the last and most puzzling of Mozart's operas is our next consideration. But before that we must consider the important effect of Mozart's masonic sympathies. That these were apparent long before he actually became a Freemason has already become obvious. He was officially admitted into freemasonry on December 14, 1784, in the *Loge zur Wohltätigkeit* (Charity), the Grand Master being Otto von Gemmingen with whom Mozart had once thought of writing a duodrama *Semiramis*. He was initiated as *Lehrlinge* (Apprentice), enthusiastically undergoing the ritual trials that were later presented in dramatic form in *The Magic Flute*. He became a truly dedicated Mason, finding here the conviction and serenity in the face of adversity and eventually death that he expressed in one of his last letters to his father, (who died less than two months later) written on April 4, 1787: 'As death, when we come to consider it closely, is the true goal of our existence, I have formed during the last few years such close relations with this best and truest friend of mankind, that his image is not only no longer terrifying to me, but is indeed very

LEFT: *Ignaz von Born (1742–91), the eminent scientist and Freemason said to be the model for Sarastro*

soothing and consoling, and I thank my God for graciously granting me the opportunity (you know what I mean) of learning that death is the key which unlocks the door to our true happiness.' He was initiated to the second degree of *Geselle* (Journeyman) in March 1785, to that of *Meister* (Master) in April. He went no further than this, the higher ranks probably beyond his ambition and capacity, but he was active in converting others to the same beliefs. His father Leopold was

33

initiated into the same lodge three months after his son, and the occasion of his elevation to Master shortly afterwards was the last time that the father and son saw each other. Mozart may also have been partly responsible for Haydn's initiation which he certainly attended in February 1785; at the *Loge zur wahren Eintracht* (True Harmony) of which Ignaz von Born, the probable inspirer of the role of Sarastro in *The Magic Flute*, was the Grand Master. The same evening Haydn went to the Mozarts' house to hear some of Mozart's quartets and made the historic remark to Leopold: 'I say to you before God and as an honest man, that your son is the greatest composer I know personally or by name.' Mozart frequently went to Born's lodge as well as his own, often in company with Schikaneder and no doubt some of the future collaboration there took tentative shape. A re-grouping of lodges at the end of 1785 found Mozart a member of the *Loge zur neugekrönten Hoffnung* (Hope Newly Crowned) where his Master was now Gebler, the librettist of *Thamos*. Among other masonic friends were his brother-in-law Josef Lange who painted the famous half-finished portrait of the composer in 1782–3, his publisher Carlo Artaria and Johann Michael Puchberg, famed as the man from whom Mozart constantly borrowed money.

From the moment of his induction Mozart wrote music for masonic purposes. Two adagios, K410 and 411 were probably designed for masonic processions; the masonic triple-knocking theme is softly introduced in the latter. These have been dated by Einstein as of 1783 but it seems more likely that they were written in 1784 after Mozart had joined his lodge. The cantata '*Dir, Seele des Weltalls*' of 1783 was commissioned for a masonic function to which non-members were invited. The first piece known to be written after he was a Mason was the *Gesellenreise Freimaurerlied*, a setting of a text by Franz Joseph von Ratschky designed to welcome members upon attaining the second degree of membership (Journeyman). The manuscript is dated March 26, 1785, around the time that he was himself initiated as a Journeyman and his father as an Apprentice. The Cantata '*Die Maurerfreude*' was composed in April 1785 in honour of Ignaz Born, Grand Master of the Lodge of True Harmony to a text by Franz Petran. It is in the key of E-flat, a key which Einstein has described as 'both heroic and mild—humane'. It is the key (with its relative C-minor) in which Mozart wrote most of his masonic music and which he used prominently in *The Magic Flute*.

One of the most effective and moving elegies in musical form was the *Maurerische Trauermusik* (masonic funeral music) which Mozart wrote for the memorial services to Duke Georg August of Mecklenburg-Strelitz and Count Franz Esterhazy von Galantha in November 1785. The music, sixty-nine bars in all, is written for a small orchestra of three bassett horns, contrabassoon, two oboes, clarinet and strings. It is almost religious music in secular terms, solemn and reverent on the one hand, with (typical of Mozart) an ingenious piece of wind writing using the lower registers of the instruments to give a dark hue to the music. It opens with heavy chords in C-minor. The oboes and clarinets later joined by the whole of the wind play a solemn chorale in slow march time. The piece ends triumphantly with a chord in the obligatory E-flat major. The Viennese masonic fraternity could count themselves fortunate to have a resident composer of the calibre of Mozart. With his fluency of output he was easily able to supply short pieces as required, such as the song *'Zerfliesset heut', geliebte Brüder'* written for the inauguration of the new lodge Hope Newly Crowned; and *'Ihre unsre neuen Leiter'* written to welcome the newly elected Grand Master of the united lodges. Both were for tenor, male choir and organ and to texts by Augustin Veith Edler von Schittlersberg.

The large question of the conflicting influences of the Catholic Church and freemasonry on Mozart's outlook and creative output needs very careful dissection. In his fascinating book *The Magic Flute, Masonic Opera*, Jacques Chailley, with commendable zeal, takes his detective work to the point of finding meaning in almost every note of the opera. Most people, even Freemasons, will not find it possible to follow him this far each time they hear the opera and the cynic may well find some of his conclusions stretching the point a little. But this is a fault common to all musical analysts. If we accept that the composer wrote far more spontaneously than this; the scholar is then free to link the impulsive actions of creation with the Freudian associations that gave them birth and, at these deeper layers, Chailley's inferences are doubtless correct. Some may find it harder to accept his constant hint, also found elsewhere, that under the inspiration of the masonic ideals his music took on a depth of feeling and meaning that the Church had never inspired. But if this argument is countered by the evidence of the tremendous amount of splendid church music that Mozart wrote before he became a Mason, it is probably equally true to say that something of the masonic spirit was always part of his make-up. Almost paradoxically the music that was written ostensibly for the Church is often far more secular and in the baroque styling of the period than those pieces which have been given a masonic connection. Anyone meeting the earliest piece we have mentioned, the '*De profundis clamavi*' must be impressed by the direct and incredibly moving simplicity of the music. In no way could Mozart have been involved in masonry at fifteen but in turning to the choral works he wrote after he had been initiated, we find this same inspired simplicity and spine-tingling beauty as in the exquisite '*Ave verum corpus*' of 1791, actually written for a school choir but filled with Mozart's most elevated convictions. The two cantatas with more specific masonic import '*Die ihr des unermesslichen Weltalls Schöpfer ehrt*' written in the summer of 1791 and '*Laut verkünde uns're Freude*' (specifically named '*Eine kleine Freimaurer Kantate*') with text by Schikaneder, are most clearly linked with the *The Magic Flute* vein. As a coda to this there is the fragment '*Lasst uns mit geschlungen Händen*' ('*Anhang zum Schluss der Freimaurerloge*') also written in the last three weeks of his life, which is almost too poignant to bear. Nobody goes so far as to claim the last great *Requiem* as masonic music but its mighty spirit (in those parts which Mozart completed) could perhaps be seen, however fancifully, as a combination of the spiritual forces of the Church and freemasonry at last reconciled.

In summary it seems safe to assume that Mozart, although brought up to be a practising Roman Catholic, had within him, throughout his life, the masonic ideals. The Church of the day, with its politics and intrigues, its dogmas and zealous laws, treated Mozart badly and probably drove him toward his final convictions. He was a creative being of supreme achievement whose true love was music but who found himself caught up in a tangled web of religious and political intrigue. He discovered in freemasonry a society claiming to be based on the most fundamental religious beliefs, the most essential belief being that of benevolent brotherhood. It has always incurred most hostility because of the secrecy, to which all members are sworn, that surrounds its rituals founded on the allegories and

RIGHT: *Joseph II who was sympathetic to the Freemasons*

symbols that are the basis of its moral code. Beyond this it functions openly, its membership and meeting-places known and its proceedings publicized in annual reports. In Mozart's time freemasonry was rarely anti-religious, being tolerant of a man's faith, but it was pushed into the position of being anti-clerical. The Roman Catholic Church held that Freemasonry was a deistic and pagan religion and that its oaths and secrecy were unlawful in the eyes of the Church. Pope Clement XII proclaimed in 1738 that Catholics who joined masonic lodges were guilty of sin and subject to ex-communication, and Pope Benedict XIV upheld this attitude. There was no secular law then against the organization. Protestant churches also found freemasonry at odds with their established orders. The

Freemasons wisely thwarted political wrath by making it openly known that they welcomed applicants of all denominations and never asked them to give up their religious beliefs.

The situation in Austria in Mozart's time was complicated by a conflict in royal circles. The Empress Maria Theresa was violently anti-masonic but her position was complicated by the fact that her husband and consort had been admitted to the order at The Hague in 1731 at the instigation of the English Ambassador, Lord Chesterfield. It was through the Emperor's affiliation that the bull of Clement XII was suppressed. In 1764, however, the Empress's tolerance gave out and Freemasonry was made illegal and was forced to operate in secrecy. On her death in 1780 it was allowed into the open again as her successor Joseph II, although never actually a mason himself, found himself mainly in sympathy with its ideals. It was hardly an unconnected train of events when Mozart, unceremoniously dismissed from the services of the unpleasant and intolerant Archbishop Hieronymus Colloredo of Salzburg in 1781, joined the Freemasons in 1784. The Emperor, still taking a benevolent interest, and perhaps making the situation more manageable, was responsible for having the eight existing lodges in Vienna merged into three larger ones in 1786. But by 1790 Leopold II had succeeded to the throne and not only confirmed Maria Theresa's active warfare against the movement but was consistently hostile to Mozart and his music. Actual persecution and punishment of Freemasons began again in 1794.

In considering the story and the music of *The Magic Flute* in subsequent chapters, it would be making matters unnecessarily involved to follow in detail the tortuous paths of Jacques Chailley already encompassed in a fascinating book. They will be looked at in a factual and musical light respectively. But a consideration of *The Magic Flute*, with its unusual and profound nature, could hardly be made without a knowledge of its masonic background which explains, to some extent, how a work written with Mozart's usual haste and fluency, could contain so many undercurrents of meaning. Mozart remained a devout but enlightened Roman Catholic but found no inconsistency in being a Freemason as well. It provided him with a moral courage and a preparation for death that his religious beliefs only partly provided. No appreciation of *The*

Magic Flute would really be complete, no real understanding of the particular nature of its music possible, without an awareness of the music that Mozart wrote as a Freemason. The affiliation brought out the finest qualities in his character and led him, in *The Magic Flute*, the *Requiem* and other late masterpieces to write some of his most sublime and noble music. The hints to be found in our glimpses of his previous operatic experiences explain the purely musical shape of his thoughts. The unique qualities of *The Magic Flute* are the outcome of Mozart's deeper beliefs being almost farcically intermingled with the curious circumstances of its creation.

The Opera's Composition

In examining the actual period of creation of *The Magic Flute* we are always doomed to failure in one important respect—i.e., in having little insight into Mozart's working method or even much knowledge of how he would have proceeded to produce this major operatic masterpiece in a period of time extending from somewhere in early June 1791 to its first performance on September 30 in the *Theater auf der Wieden*. If that seems a miraculously short period of time, even with our acceptance of Mozart's fecundity, it is made even more bemusing by knowing that on June 18 he composed the *Ave verum corpus* motet for his choirmaster friend Anton Stell and the masonic cantata K619 mentioned earlier, had to take time off *The Magic Flute* to complete *La Clemenza di Tito* (*The Clemency of Titus*) for its performance on September 6 and that, on September 28, he not only noted in his diary that he had completed *The Magic Flute* overture but the Clarinet Concerto as well. And he was already working on the *Requiem*.

In practical terms Mozart was in a state of crisis. He was a sick man himself and work was not exactly helped by the well-meant friendship of Schikaneder who was inclined to drag him off to heavy drinking sessions while still expecting the opera to be completed. Constanze was pregnant and unwell and was in Baden taking the cure so Mozart tried to go and see her as often as possible. However his musical fertility was undiminished and 1790 had been a creative year in spite of the unhelpful disapproval of Leopold II which barred him from any remunerative musical post. His income from a few pupils and the uncertain payment for works commissioned in those pre-copyright days was negligible and he only made ends meet by borrowing from masonic friends. So, when Schikaneder asked him to collaborate on a work for his theatre and company, a combination of his still burning desire to write a German opera and the conviction of his own capabilities in this direction,

41

ABOVE LEFT: *Playbill for the first performance of* The Magic Flute *on September 30, 1791 at the* Theater auf der Wieden

ABOVE RIGHT: *Title-page of the first edition of the libretto*

loyalty to an old masonic friend, and the simple need of cash made him accept the offer without hesitation.

Schikaneder had been a friend of Mozart and his family from around 1780 when his company had visited Salzburg. Coming from a poor background, he had started out as an itinerant musician and actor and had married the foster daughter of Andreas Schopf in whose theatrical company he had played. Born in 1751, he had made a good reputation as an actor by 1775 and was well known for his portrayal of Shakespearean tragic roles such as Hamlet, Macbeth and King Lear. There was a particularly triumphant *Hamlet* in Munich in 1778, and, in the same year, he wrote his first successful opera *Die Lyranten*. In 1778 he was with Joseph Moser's company playing in opera and classical drama and, being offered the company, gave up a proffered engagement with the Munich Opera and bought it. It was with this company that he visited Salzburg and first met

Mozart. By 1784 *The Seraglio* was in the company's repertoire. Schikaneder was favourably noticed by Joseph II who invited him to Vienna, where, with the disbanding of the German Opera and a repertoire that in no way clashed with the Italian Opera company, he was able to hold sway in the field of national opera and drama. He disbanded his company in 1785, at which time his wife left him for Johann Friedel who was soon to become director of the *Theater auf der Wieden* in the suburbs of

LEFT: *Emanuel Schikaneder (1751–1812), the librettist of* The Magic Flute

Vienna. Schikaneder was granted permission to build a *singspiel* theatre in Vienna but found himself unable to raise the finances and in 1786 continued with a new touring company. They included Salzburg in their itinerary and in 1787 visited Regensburg where Schikaneder joined a masonic lodge and thus took the first unknowing steps toward *The Magic Flute* saga. He was not an ideal Mason and was, in fact, expelled from the Regensburg lodge for unbecoming behaviour, but he was allowed to remain attached to various other lodges and found the association useful in his career. In 1789 Johann Friedel died and Schikaneder's wife asked him to come and help her run the *Theater auf der Wieden*. He seems to have been of a forgiving character and agreed to do so, running a *singspiel* company there with the financial help of a fellow-mason Joseph von Bauernfeld who was later connected with Schubert as a translator of Shakespeare into German.

The *Theater auf der Wieden* was a temporary structure which held a thousand people and included accommodation for the company and staff. It was later replaced as Vienna's opera house by the *Theater an der Wien* (with which it is sometimes confused) which was built on an entirely different site in 1801. Its main repertoire was comic *singspiel*, much favoured by the Viennese audiences of the day, and a species of near-pantomime spectacles involving animals and magic spells that were the obvious forerunner of *The Magic Flute*. These included *Oberon* with music by Paul Wranitzky (from which Mozart borrowed) using the same story that Weber used later; and *Der Stein der Weisen* (*The Philosopher's Stone*) with music by Benedikt Schack some of which was scored by Mozart—and which was the motivating inspiration of the Schikaneder-Mozart collaboration.

Der Stein der Weisen was taken from a book of fairy-tales from the East called *Dschinnistan*. The particular story used was set in Egypt and involved a hero who had to undergo trials by fire and water. It was by A. L. Leibskind and was called *Lulu, oder die Zauberflöte*. *Oberon* had included a magic horn, but Schack had omitted the magic flute element in *Lulu* and it was this omission that gave Schikaneder the idea of taking that part of the story to squeeze yet another *singspiel* from this source.

In brief, the synopsis upon which Schikaneder worked was a story in which Prince Lulu, son of the King of Khurashan, is

OPPOSITE:
Metropolitan Opera production 1912–13; Bella Alten as Papagena and Otto Goritz as Papageno

45

sent by the good fairy Perifirime to rescue her daughter Sidi from the clutches of the evil wizard Dilsengbuin. He is given a magic flute which can transform him into any guise or place a charm on any man or animal. In spite of the wizard's wiles Lulu escapes with Sidi, and Perifirime destroys the wizard's castle.

The prototypes for Tamino, Pamina, the Queen and Sarastro were thus provided. Schikaneder, wanting a good comic part for himself, invented Papageno on the basis of a character in *Oberon* and the bird-catcher Truffaldino from a comedy *Il re cervo*. The comic in feathers and a bird's beak had long been a stock figure in the *commedia dell'arte*. Schikaneder's fertile imagination wrought other changes. The good fairy became the wicked Queen of the Night while the wicked wizard became the idealistic masonic figure of Sarastro. The genii who guided Tamino and Papageno in their quest for Pamina were taken from another story in the fairy-tale collection called *The Three Boys*. A masonic implication exists already in this story in which the hero is told to be 'steadfast, patient and taciturn'. For other twists and touches in the story Schikaneder drew from his memories of numerous dramas and operas, including some of Mozart's and gradually evolved his plot. It seems beyond question that the intent to draw upon the symbolism and ideals of freemasonry was there at the very beginning of Schikaneder's and Mozart's discussions, doubtless carried on in various convivial lodges and taverns. Some of the masonic material he appears to have drawn from a French novel *Sethos* by Jean Terrasson which attempts to forge a link between freemasonry and its ancient Egyptian origins. A further source of inspiration is one only covered with significant emphasis in Janos Liebner's book *Mozart on the Stage* and almost totally ignored by other commentators; that is the close knowledge of Shakespeare that Schikaneder possessed. Liebner draws convincing parallels between *The Magic Flute* and *The Tempest* and indeed the superficial resemblance strikes many people on a first acquaintance with the opera, the links with Oberon and Sarastro, Papageno and Caliban, most obvious in the first confrontations of Papageno and Tamino and in the general setting of both works. It is certainly an interesting parallel, if nothing more.

At this point the great mystery of *The Magic Flute*'s creation creeps in. It is fairly generally accepted that, at a point where

46

Mozart had got into writing the Act I finale, he and Schikaneder decided to change the whole nature of the opera; transforming it from a simple comic *singspiel*, practically a pantomime, into the serious, but curiously mixed opera that it became. It may have been at this stage that even deeper masonic significance was imposed; where the Queen of the Night became the villain of the piece instead of the good fairy, and where Sarastro took on his benevolent role. Certainly the character of the music in Act I is of a far lighter and less noble character than it takes on, for instance, with the introduction of the Three Boys who are a clear masonic symbol. It starts, in other words, as if it was purely a straightforward musical version of the *Lulu* cum *Magic Flute* story with (as is noted later in the synopsis) even the character of the Queen of the Night totally ambiguous. At this point she could well be the heroine of the piece rather than the 'villainess'. Was this simply a clever piece of dramatic plot-building or did the collaborators change the opera but, in their haste, fail to re-write the first act. Was Mozart's music, so far, left intact or was some of that re-written? There are strong reasons given for supposing that the nature of the opera was wholly changed. Firstly, and the most substantial, that in June 1791, just as *The Magic Flute* was in its first stages, Marinelli produced in Vienna a magical comic opera called *Kaspar der Fagottist, oder Die Zauberzither* which was also based on *Lulu*. Its characters are renamed but the plot is essentially the same. It is known that Mozart saw the opera and thought it both noisy and stupid.

This could hardly have left Mozart unaffected. Beyond which, the sublime music that he had already written, which he knew was some of his best (and which he died still loving and savouring), must by now have made him wish to make this work something more than a mere comic pantomime. Maybe the serious masonic side had begun to impose itself upon both composer and librettist and the whole thing simply grew upon them willy nilly. The very nature of *The Magic Flute* suggests that it turned into a great opera from simple beginnings; that Mozart, drawing on the resources that freemasonry had given him and the music he had already been inspired to write on its behalf now knew that this side of the work had to be represented as well. On the other hand, having found such a superb comic vein for Papageno he was not going to let that be discarded and was quite content, as was his nature and as he had done in *Don Giovanni*, to let the sublime and the comic live happily side by side. His commitment to masonry, and Schikaneder's also, if in a lesser degree, were probably the over-riding influences—not the conflicting production of *Kaspar*. Indeed, if we want to be mystical, we may read into the inspiring influences behind *The Magic Flute* the hand of God (or Isis and Osiris); for such magical creativeness is not solely a matter of sordid practicality. Mozart himself felt very much the same following the mysterious commission for a Requiem mass which eventually became his own.

BELOW: *The summer house in the grounds of the* Freihaus *theatre where Mozart worked on the score of the opera*

Such matters seem likely to remain beyond definite proof one way or the other. So does the mysterious complication of another possible hand in the creation of *The Magic Flute*. This is mainly examined in Edward J. Dent's *Mozart's Operas* but has been allowed to lie fallow since. Dent turns our attention to a book *Die Opern in Deutschland* written by Julius Cornet in 1849 which reports a meeting in Vienna in 1818 with a dignified old gentleman named C. L. Giesecke who had been a member of the Schikaneder chorus. By this time he had become a distinguished professor in the University of Dublin. He had also been a Freemason. He claimed that he was the real author of *The Magic Flute* and that Schikaneder's only contribution had been the creation of the figures of Papageno and Papagena, the former for his own portrayal.

Some of the statements given to help prove this claim in Cornet's book are inaccurate but nevertheless Giesecke (whose real name at the time of the events involved with Johann Georg Metzler) was certainly around at the time and was involved in the production of the aforementioned *Oberon*. Queries naturally arose as to why he did not claim his authorship earlier. In fact, it seems that he did, for mention is made in a preface to a Schikaneder play published in 1794 that a theatrical journalist has been impertinent enough to claim co-authorship of *The Magic Flute*. Giesecke left Vienna at about this time, perhaps in regard for his safety as a mason, though Schikaneder managed to survive the new laws. Whether this was the rather more serious hand that transformed *The Magic Flute* from a pantomime to a serious masonic opera, may someday be resolved by further close scholarship. Many writers, notably the Viennese ones, have damned his claims. It makes no jot of difference to the resulting opera, but it is a fascinating area for speculation.

To return to partial facts. It is reported that Schikaneder put a little summerhouse in the courtyard of the *Freihaus* theatre (long worshipped as a venerated shrine) at Mozart's disposal. Here he could work comfortably in the summer months and be in close contact with his collaborator. 'If it all turns out a fiasco.' warned Mozart, 'it will not be my fault, for I have never written a magic opera in my life.' A further pleasant but probably false legend (considering the season of the year) was that Schikaneder fed Mozart on oysters and wine. Other people claim that it was

Salieri who tried to poison him! Mozart stayed at night with other friends, including Schikaneder, and, for certain periods, in a tavern in Kahlenberg. By July 2 he was ready to put the finishing touches to the full score of Act I, the rough work having been done by his pupil Sussmayr. The cast were already studying the vocal lines. His child, Franz Xaver—one of the only two who survived—was born on July 26 and Wolfgang and Constanze went to Prague to see the premiere of *La Clemenza di Tito*. They returned in mid-September and Mozart worked assiduously on the rest of the score, leaving the Overture to the last.

Synopsis of the Plot

The opera is in two acts. The setting of Act One, Scene One is a rocky desert in Egypt, the country from which freemasonry is believed to have originated. There is a constant ambiguity in the setting, as in most aspects of the opera, in that we are also in a kingdom of legend and fantasy—the kingdom of the Queen of the Night. These ambiguities probably arise from the hurried change of the character of the opera from a straightforward pantomime to an opera glorifying freemasonry. Thus we also find that the first character to appear, Tamino, was originally dressed in what is usually described as a Japanese hunting-jacket (in some texts Javanese) and is specified by some commentators, again without obvious significance, as being a Japanese (or Javanese) Prince. He has rarely been portrayed as an Oriental in subsequent productions. The actual settings of each scene can be authentically described from Schikaneder's original sketches. The rocky desert, relieved by a few desultory trees, has a distant vista of hills. In the centre a ruined temple.

Tamino enters pursued by a large serpent. He has carelessly left himself in the position of having a bow but no arrows and the serpent is about to pounce. With a desperate cry for help he is overcome by exhaustion and falls unconscious. In the very nick of time three veiled ladies, dressed in black, each with a silver spear, enter and slay the serpent, commending their own bravery. The ladies, servants of the Queen of the Night, gaze upon Tamino and comment on his handsome features, and each one suggests that she should be the one to stay and watch over him while the other two convey the news of his arrival to the Queen. Unable to resolve this point, they decide all three must go and they leave Tamino and tell the audience they will return. Some productions (as in the original) set the temple in the centre of the stage so that the characters come from it and disappear into it but others make this a later scene and have the characters depart for a more distant location.

Tamino now stirs and is astonished to find the serpent lying dead beside him. He wonders whether he has been dreaming or if some high power has intervened. As he recovers he sees a strange figure approaching playing a pipe. He hides behind a tree. It is Papageno, the bird-catcher, dressed in a suit of feathers and carrying on his back a cage almost as big as himself containing various birds. In a pleasant folky kind of song (*Der Vogelfänger bin ich ja*) he explains his occupation and skills; how he is renowned for his ability to lure birds into his trap with his piping. He would much prefer to have the same ability to lure maidens. Having caught a score of them he would choose the fairest and bribe her with sugar (in modern terms, perhaps a box of chocolates) and then, he muses, they would kiss and lie down together and he would sing her a lullaby.

Tamino ventures to call out 'Hey there!' at which Papageno starts and asks who is there. They introduce themselves,

ABOVE: *Stage set for an early production showing Papageno confronted by the Three Ladies while boasting to Tamino over the serpent's death*

53

Tamino admitting to being a Prince whose father rules over many lands. Papageno is astonished to hear that there are *other* lands and people and thinks of the business he might do there. He tells of the humble hut he lives in and how he catches birds for the Queen and her Ladies in return for food and drink. Tamino has heard of the Queen of the Night and asks if this is she and what she looks like. Papageno is contemptuous of this question. What mortal can see the Queen of the Night? Tamino deserves to be caught in Papageno's basket and be taken to her to be cooked like the other birds. Tamino glares threateningly at Papageno and says that he looks like a bird himself, at which Papageno, a thorough coward, blusters that he has the strength of ten. So it was you who killed the serpent, says Tamino. Papageno notices the serpent, with some alarm, for the first time and opportunely accepts the credit for the deed. Such is his strength (he says) that, without a weapon he was able to strangle it. Unfortunately for Papageno the three veiled Ladies appear at this moment and he knows he is in trouble. Tamino asks who they are and if they are very beautiful. Papageno makes things worse for himself by saying that if they were beautiful they would not need to veil their faces. Immediate retribution follows: instead of wine he gets water, instead of food a stone and he has a padlock clamped on his mouth so that he can tell no more lies. The Ladies turn to Tamino and tell him that they slew the serpent but that he need not fear them, joy and ecstasy await him. They give him a portrait which the Queen has sent. It is of her daughter and if the portrait pleases him he has a great future in store. Tamino is left alone to contemplate the picture which, in the aria *Dies Bildnis ist bezaubernd schön*, he finds of surpassing beauty. He falls in love with the vision. Just to be with her would make him feel warm and pure. He longs to embrace her and make her his for ever.

The three Ladies reappear and tell him how the Queen has been greatly pleased at hearing his words and hopes that his bravery is as great as his tenderness. She has chosen him to save her daughter Pamina whom the wicked demon Sarastro has snatched away. He lives in a closely guarded castle in the mountains. Tamino swears to save her; at which, to his alarm, the mountains part and the Queen of the Night appears. She bids him to have no fear (*O zitt're nicht, mein lieber Sohn!*) for it is on his purity and innocence that she relies to rescue her only

child from the clutches of the evil fiend who stole her. Unable to defeat his powers she looks to Tamino to save her and as reward offers Pamina's hand in marriage. The Queen disappears and the mountains close.

Once more Tamino is alone and wonders if it is all a dream. He meets Papageno again but conversation proves fruitless as the bird-catcher still has the padlock on his mouth and Tamino can do nothing about it. The three Ladies return to say that the Queen has pardoned Papageno for the time being and the padlock is removed with the warning that he must tell no more lies. Papageno readily agrees and joins sanctimoniously with the Ladies and Tamino in the moral refrain 'If only all liars had their mouths padlocked, then, instead of hate and lies and slander, men would live with love and brotherhood'. The first Lady now presents Tamino with a magic flute which will protect him whenever evil assails him. With it he can do wonderful things— change men's passions, despair to joy, old bachelors to young lovers, increase mankind's happiness. At this point Papageno

ABOVE: *Papageno with the padlock clamped on his mouth in a British National Opera production of 1922*

RIGHT: *Geraint Evans as Papageno with his chiming bells in the 1962 Covent Garden production*

RIGHT: *Geraint Evans as Papageno with his chiming bells in the 1962 Covent Garden production*

considers it time for him to depart while he is in good shape, but the Ladies tell him that the Queen has commanded that he shall go with Tamino to find Sarastro. Papageno politely declines having no wish to be flayed and roasted by Sarastro, but the Ladies are insistent and tell him that the Prince will look after him if he acts as his servant. Papageno is not at all pleased at the command but is given as a present a little musical instrument with a set of chiming bells. He is assured that he will be able to play it, and that they will both be protected by the combination of flute and bells. Papageno (somewhat surprisingly) asks how they will find the way to Sarastro's castle and they are told that they will be accompanied by three young, beautiful and wise youths, the genii of the flute, who will lead the way and whose commands they must always obey. They bid the Ladies farewell and set off on their journey.

At this point we might take a first objective view of *The Magic Flute* and the situation and characters so far presented. As remarked in the previous chapter, the change from a simple pantomime to masonic opera was perhaps done hurriedly and imperfectly. Whether deliberately or accidentally we are for the moment left in some doubt as to the dramatic and moral implications of the characters depicted. There is nothing so far that makes us accept the Queen of the Night as anything but a figure of goodness and right. She has been wronged and Sarastro has been labelled the wicked monster against which she fights. She and her Ladies have saved Tamino, even if for their own ends, and they have been portrayed in a benevolent light, their only harsh act the justifiable punishment of Papageno for telling lies. Sarastro, only by mention and implication, has been branded the villain of the piece. But we must take the hint offered by the name of the Queen, described by Papageno as *'sternflammende'* (star-radiant), by the Ladies as the 'great Queen', for it is not an accident that she is the 'Queen of the Night' and her Ladies dressed in black; both blackness and the powers of night being immemorially associated with evil. Neither does the situation really explain why the Queen, who can split mountains asunder and proffer magic flutes, should be incapable of dealing with a mere magician herself without the aid of an incompetent warrior like Tamino who runs around without arrows to his bow. Good must always overcome evil in our folk-legends, so we must take that as a hint of who is on which side. It may simply be a false clue that it is the Ladies who prompt the first moral statement in the opera about brotherhood and love. However much we would like to take *The Magic Flute* as an opera full of good music but an absurd libretto, we are bound to take heed of the commentators who find reflections of reality in it, allegory and freemasonry. Early writers from around the mid-nineteenth century were already identifying its characters with real people that Schikaneder and Mozart might have enjoyed criticizing or praising. Tamino has been identified with the Emperor Joseph II whom they saw as a saviour of the Austrian people, represented by Pamina, and who had many good things to his credit like encouraging Mozart to write an opera, ideas of establishing German opera in Vienna, dissolving monastic establishments and a sympathetic interest in freemasonry in spite of the efforts of one Leopold Aloys Hoffmann, a traitorous Freemason who tried to persuade him that the Masons were organizing a revolution. At this point we have not yet met Monostatos, the natural villain, who might well have represented Hoffmann in particular, or the whole group of Jesuits and other religious orders in general. The Queen of the Night was meant to represent the scheming Maria Therese who was totally hostile to freemasonry; and perhaps by implication the religiously influenced Establishment of the time. Sarastro was said to represent Ignaz von Born, the prominent Freemason and an eminent scientist, who would be something of a hero to his fellow-spirits.

However, let the plot unfold and thicken. The scene now moves to a room in Sarastro's palace, richly furnished in the best Egyptian fashions of the day. And now we meet Monostatos, Sarastro's brutal henchman, a Moor of the sergeant-major type who enjoys a bit of brutality but is basically portrayed as a faintly comic character. He is enjoying a moment when he has Pamina in his power; a true pantomime villain to be hissed at by the audience. Hinting that her end is nigh, he has her bound by slaves and, sending them away, is obviously intent on rape, at least. Pamina swoons. However, like all true

BELOW: *Queen of the Night: One of the famous designs by Karl Friedrich Schinkel (1781–1841) for the Berlin production of 1816*

pantomime villains, he is a fool and a coward and when Papageno suddenly enters in his outlandish costume he mistakes him for the devil and takes to his heels. Papageno, not quite sure where he is, is not less startled at his first sighting of a black face but philosophises that if there are black birds then why shouldn't there be black men. He sees Pamina, recovering from her faint, recognises her from the portrait and explains that he is an envoy from the 'star-radiant' Queen. He tells her of the Prince who has been appointed by her mother to rescue her and that the Prince has fallen in love with her. What has kept him so long, asks Pamina with typical practicality. Papageno explains that he has been sent in advance to herald Tamino's arrival. Pamina warns him of what Sarastro will do to him if he is caught but Papageno's imagination is not lacking in this direction. Pamina asks him if he has a wife waiting for him to which Papageno sadly replies in the negative. Pamina assures him that Heaven will eventually find him the wife he wants and in a gentle duet, '*Bei Männern, welche Liebe fühlen*', they reassure each other that lovers must always obtain happiness in the end and that love is the pleasantest thing in the world. Nothing is nobler or more ennobling than true marriage. (This scene might well have been left intact from Schikaneder's original pantomime scheme, combining as it does farce, melodrama and sentiment and the ages-old theme of 'it's love that makes the world go round'. Enriched by Mozart's music, it provides a pleasant interlude.)

A transformation now to a grove where stand three beautiful temples. On the centre one are inscribed the words 'Temple of Wisdom'; connected to it by a colonnade the one on the right is inscribed 'Temple of Reason', the one on the left 'Temple of Nature'. The Three Boys lead in Tamino explaining that this is the path that leads him to his goal and that he must be steadfast, patient and discreet. When he asks if he will find Pamina here they repeat their admonition and say that if he behaves as a man then as man he will triumph. They leave him and he reflects ('*Die Weisheitslehre dieser Knaben*') on the wisdom of the boys and wonders what knowledge lies behind the inscriptions on the temples. Bolstered by his noble purpose and clear conscience he decides to enter and to save Pamina. He tries the temple on the right but a voice forbids his entry. Likewise when he tries the temple on the left. He knocks on the door of

ABOVE: *The brutal Monostatos threatens Pamina (1922 British National Opera Company production).*

the centre temple and a priest appears and asks him what he wants. When Tamino replies that he desires love and virtue's just reward, the priest praises his lofty ideals but asks how can he expect to find these when death and vengeance are uppermost in his mind. Tamino replies that his vengeance is only directed to the evil fiend Sarastro. The priest tells him that Sarastro is no tyrant or sorcerer, as the Queen has misled him into believing, but a man of noble character who dwells in the temple of wisdom and is their respected ruler. The priest tells him that he will learn Sarastro's purpose and whether Pamina is alive and safe only when he extends the hand of friendship and swears an eternal bond in the holy place. This solemn dialogue concluded the priest departs and Tamino is left to query, in a profound recitative. (*'O ewige Nacht!'*)—When will the eternal night end? When will light come to him? A chorus from within the temple softly answers—soon or nevermore. Does Pamina live? When he is told she does he offers thanks and takes out his magic flute and asks the gods to give him power to express his gratitude in the sweetest possible strains. He plays and all the strange animals of the forest come out and listen to him. When he stops playing they immediately flee. He realises the strength of the flute's magic; that it can even charm the wild beasts ('*Wie stark ist nich dein Zauberton*'). But his one great desire is now to find Pamina. As he asks where she is, he hears Papageno's pipe within and blows his flute. Again Papageno replies and Tamino rushes off to find him.

Pamina and Papageno enter swift of foot and bold of heart ('*Schnelle Füsse, rascher Mut*') anxious to find Tamino. Pamina calls and Papageno tootles his pipe and now Tamino answers from within on his flute. They are overjoyed to know that he is

LEFT: *In Vienna State Opera productions members of the Vienna Boys' Choir always take the parts of the Three Boys*

61

so near and Papageno asks him to come swiftly. But the evil Monostatos enters and mocks her. He orders the slaves to bind the pair with chains and they fear that their quest is at an end. But Papageno remembers in time that he has the magic chime of bells at his disposal. He turns the handle of his little machine and the Moor and his servants are captivated by the music. They cannot resist its command and are forced to dance and sing and thus depart. As Papageno and Pamina rejoice at their escape and bless the magic benevolence of the bells, they hear voices hailing the glory of Sarastro. They tremble and shiver at the thought of what Sarastro might do to them. Papageno wishes he was a mouse. Pamina decides that the best thing they can do is tell the simple truth.

The comedy of the Pamina, Papageno, Monostatos scene is transformed by Pamina's sincere words. Sarastro now enters with his followers singing a solemn chorus in his praise. Pamina kneels before him and confesses that she tried to escape from his domain but only because the wicked Moor had tried to seduce her. Sarastro is kind and understanding. He knows of her great love which he does not condemn but says he cannot set her free. She pleads that her love as a daughter urges her to return home; but Sarastro has a good old-fashioned reply to this. He tells her that a man must be her master, for without a man a woman could never fulfil her aim in life.

Monostatos now drags in Tamino, and he and Pamina meet for the first time with instant recognition and love. They embrace. Monostatos is indignant at their insolence and drags them apart. He kneels to Sarastro and denounces Tamino and Papageno who tried to steal Pamina away. Expecting praise he is sentenced, in spite of his protestations, to a flogging of seventy-seven lashes. The chorus praise Sarastro who both rewards and punishes with justice. Sarastro commands that the two lovers be brought into the Temple of Ordeals, their heads covered, so that they can be purified and be proved worthy of the higher happiness. When virtue and true justice reign throughout the world, the chorus conclude solemnly, then Heaven on earth will be discovered and men and gods will be united.

By this stage the ambiguity has been more or less resolved. We are already on the side of Sarastro, although the suggestion of ruthless power has not been entirely removed. At this point we

ABOVE: *The Moor and his servants are spellbound by Papageno's magic pipes in a 1962 Sadler's Wells production*

are left, as those outside the secrets of freemasonry are still left, with lingering doubts as to the true nature of any organization that needs to function in such a secretive manner. The librettists have given us every assurance as to the wisdom and high ideals of the movement but perhaps we already sense that *The Magic Flute* is going to deprive us of the culminating insight.

Act II begins in a grove of palms outside the Temple. To a solemn march Sarastro and the Priests enter. Sarastro explains the nature of the occasion, 'the greatest day of our time as Tamino, son of a king, waits at the North door of the Temple to tear off the veil of darkness and gaze upon the light of the gods Isis and Osiris.' It is their duty to watch over this virtuous youth and offer him the hand of friendship. It is asked and confirmed that he has virtue and reticence and is rich in good deeds. Sarastro then gives thanks that the gods have ordained the gentle and virtuous maid Pamina for this youth. It was for this reason that Sarastro took her from the Queen of the Night, a vain woman who bemuses her people with trickery and superstition and plots to destroy the temple of freemasonry. That she shall never do and Tamino will help to defend it. But will Tamino be able to stand the stern trials that await him? He is a Prince and a man and his wisdom is honoured. Sarastro commands that Tamino and his friends be brought into the courtyard and that the Priest make them aware of the power of the gods. Sarastro prays ('*O, Isis und Osiris*') that they may be granted strength to achieve the goal of wisdom. Should they fail then grant them a place in Heaven.

In the Temple Courtyard that evening Tamino and Papageno are led in by three priests and left alone. As thunder rolls, they wonder where they are, and Papageno admits that he has cold shivers down his back. The Priests enter and ask what brings them there. Tamino answers nobly—friendship and love—for which he will fight to the death and undergo every ordeal. Papageno is not quite so enthusiastic. All he really wants is sleep, food and drink—and perhaps a wife. These he cannot have unless he submits to every command even to the point of death. Papageno thinks he might prefer to stay single. But the Priest promises that Sarastro has a maiden kept for him, just like him in dress and colour, young and beautiful and called Papagena. Papageno would like to see her and is promised that he can if he speaks no word to her. Similarly Tamino may see Pamina but must not speak to her. The Priests leave them with a warning to guard against the wiles of women ('*Bewahret euch vor Weibertücken*'); many a man has been betrayed by thoughts of love and ended in despair and death. The Priests leave them; and now the three Ladies of the Queen of the Night appear before them. The Ladies try to persuade them to give up their quest for truth and light and tell them that those who take the oath will burn in hell. But Tamino remains silent and even Papageno, with prompting from Tamino, manages to keep his mouth shut. The Ladies depart frustrated and Papageno falls exhausted with the effort of silence. The Priests return to congratulate them on passing their first test but warn them of more to come. Papageno is revived and they are led away.

The scene changes to a garden where Pamina is sleeping in an arbour of flowers, the moonlight shining on her face. Monostatos creeps in and, seeing her alone, he bemoans the fate of one like himself who feels the pangs of love ('*Alles fühlt der Liebe Freuden*') but is denied it because of a black and ugly face.

ABOVE: *Sarastro
speaks to the Priests in
the Glyndebourne
Festival production of
1978 with set designs
by David Hockney
(Thomas Thomaschke
as Sarastro, Willard
White as the
Speaker).*

Has he not a heart, is he not of flesh and blood? He asks the
moon to forgive him if he touches her white loveliness; to turn
away if she does not wish to see. We can now feel almost sorry
for poor Monostatos. Just as he is about to steal a kiss the
Queen of the Night appears and, as Pamina awakes, asks what has
become of the youth she sent to save her. Hearing he has joined
the secret band she declares him to be doomed. She gives
Pamina a dagger commanding her to kill Sarastro with it. Her
fury boils over in the aria '*Der Hölle Rache kocht in meinem Herzen*'
(A vengeful hell does pulse within my heart) and she swears a
mother's vow that Sarastro must die. She sinks out of sight.
Monastatos finds her with the dagger and threatening that he
will reveal the plot (to which Pamina has never agreed) he
demands her love in return for his silence. She refuses and he is
about to kill her when Sarastro enters and, accepting
Monostatos's claim that he only wished to save him, allows him

to go. Pamina begs Sarastro not to punish her mother who was only moved by grief. Sarastro assures her that she will be content with the punishment he decides upon and explains ('*In diesen Heil'gen Hallen*') that vengeance is not their way, but love and friendship is given to the fallen. All sins are forgiven, and this should be man's teaching. The scene changes to a vast hall where Tamino and Papageno are brought in and again reminded of their vow of silence. Papageno tries to talk about his old happy life but Tamino tries to keep him quiet. Papageno supposes he might talk to himself, at least. He is longing for a drink of water. An old crone enters and offers him a goblet of water. She says that her age is eighteen-and-two-minutes but he hardly believes this. She says that she is his own sweetheart Papagena and he is so put out that he flings the water in her face. She goes off before he is able to find out her name and he vows that from now on he will hold his tongue. The Three Boys now appear. One carries the magic flute, another the magic bells and a table appears laden with good things to eat. They encourage Tamino and Papageno to eat but when Papageno asks if he may, Tamino will only play on his flute. Pamina now comes and is over-joyed to find Tamino, but he will not speak to her and Papageno's mouth is too full for him to do so. Pamina is heart-broken and believes she has lost her love for ever ('*Ach, ich fühl's, es ist verschwunden*'). She weeps and vows that if she cannot have her love she will die.

In a vault beneath the Temple the Priests sing a solemn hymn of praise to Isis and Osiris. Tamino is led in by a Priest and then Pamina. Sarastro bids them to take their last farewell of each other. This they do in the trio '*Soll ich dich, Teurer, nicht mehr sehn?*', with Sarastro assuring them that the gods will protect them. They pray that contentment will come again. A confused Papageno tries to follow Tamino but he is ordered back. The Priest tells him that although he does not deserve it the gods have remitted his punishment but that he will never feel true divine content. Papageno is quite happy to settle for wine and one other thing—a maiden ('*Ein Mädchen oder Weibchen*') or even any woman. If only one would come to his aid with just one kiss he would be happy. At which the old crone appears and says that if he will be faithful to her for ever she will always love him. His enthusiasm wavers a little but she warns him that if he doesn't give her his hand in love he will be imprisoned here for

RIGHT: *Sadler's Wells
1955 production with
Denis Dowling as
Papageno and Marion
Studholme (heavily
disguised) as Papagena*

OPPOSITE: *Thomas
Allen as Papageno is
saved from suicide by
the Three Boys
(Covent Garden
1979).*

ever—without a sweetheart. Papageno is not yet ready to renounce the world and promises to be true to her forever—so long (aside) as he sees none fairer. At which the crone turns into a young girl dressed exactly like Papageno. It is *his* Papagena whom he joyfully embraces. But, alas, she is sent off by a Priest who says that Papageno is not yet worthy of her.

The three boy genii are heard in the garden singing of the joys of the sun ('*Bald prangt, den Morgen zu verkünden*') whose rays sweep away superstition and bring men nearer to the gods. They pity Pamina who is in a state of despair and promise to watch over her. Pamina enters with a dagger in her hand determined to end her life. As she declares she must commit

suicide the genii comfort her and finally dissuade her with tender words, promising that, although they cannot yet reveal how, they can take her and prove to her that Tamino still loves her, and she agrees to go with them.

Two great mountains are seen, one throwing out water, the other fire and two men in black armour stand waiting to lead Tamino to his final trial, the test by fire and water. Tamino refuses to waver and to his joy Pamina joins him to face death by his side (*'Ich werde aller Orten an deiner Seite sein'*). They can now speak of their love with a wisdom and serenity they had not known before. They have journeyed through the fiery furnace together and survived the menace of the water, guided by Isis, and now their faith and love is rewarded. Their strength in the face of danger means that their marriage can now be consecrated in the Temple.

Papageno's ensuing pageant of mock suicide ('*Papagena!*
Papagena! Papagena! Weibchen! Täubchen! Meine Schöne!') adds a
marvellous touch of humour and warmth after the seriousness
of the Tamino and Pamina scene. Now that his love has gone he
decides to hang himself, but (shades of Peter Pan and
Tinkerbell) if only one voice will take pity on him he will forego
the event. He hopefully counts to three but no voice intervenes.
Just as he is about to try again, the Three Boys arrive and advise
him to make the best of his one life. In his despair he had
forgotten the magic bells which they now suggest he uses to
bring his Papagena to him. He does and she appears. In the
joyful stuttering duet '*Pa-Pa-Pa-Pa-Pa-Pa-Papagena*' they sing
of their happiness and their hopes for first a little Papageno and
then a little Papagena and many more children to enjoy their
parents' blessing.

Finally, before the Temple, Monostatos enters with the
Queen of the Night and her Ladies who are still seeking revenge
on Sarastro. Monostatos demands the hand of Pamina for his
help in getting them into the Temple and the promise is made.
Within the Temple they hear a dreadful sound like thunder or a
waterfall. They prepare to enter to slay all the Priests with fire
and sword and to plunge the world into the eternal night that is
their natural element. Suddenly everything is bathed in a
great blaze of sunlight. The Queen of the Night and her retinue
disappear and Sarastro stands there exalted with Tamino and
Pamina both clothed in priestly robes surrounded by the Priests
and the Three Boys carrying sheaves of flowers. Within the
Temple of the Sun Sarastro proclaims that the golden
splendours of light have shattered the power of the evil ones.
The Priests hail the initiates and give thanks to Isis and Osiris.
They shall be crowned in glory, and wisdom and beauty shall
abound for ever. The sound of the magic flute brings the opera
to a close.

The Music

Overtures to operas should rightly be written, as the overture to *The Magic Flute* was, at the conclusion of the composer's labours on the score. As in his other operas, Mozart's overture is a symphonic resumé of the mood and action of the play with no direct quotes from anything that follows. It is scored for two flutes, two oboes, two B-flat clarinets, two bassoons, two E-flat horns, two E-flat trumpets, three trombones, timpani tuned to E-flat and B-flat, and strings. The trombones are generally given a significant part in a Mozart orchestration—they were effectively used in *Idomeneo*, *Don Giovanni* and in the *Requiem* to come—and in *The Magic Flute* can be said to characterize the voices of Isis and Osiris. The overture is in the key of E-flat, the predominant key of the opera (and of all Mozart's masonic music), emotionally solid and solemn but also, particularly in brass terms, bold and brilliant. There is even a significance to be found in the three flats of the key signature—i.e., the important symbolic 'three' which pursues us throughout the opera; the traditional three knocks, the three grades of masonry, and, in this particular story, the Three Boys and the Three Ladies. Just as three chords in C-minor started the first instrumental section of *King Thamos* so, in a sense, they do here, though the second and third sustained minim chords in E-flat, C-minor and E-flat are given a pre-echoing semi-quaver chord. But this still gives the effect of *three* solemn knocks, although Chailley accepts it as five (associated with female initiation and hence the domain of the Queen of the Night, which, in view of her final role, seems rather out of keeping). As if to emphasize the solemn aspect that the opera has taken on during its conception Mozart continues the adagio introduction with a truly hymn-like, solemn yet melodious theme weighted in the fifth and seventh bars with *fp* chord from the woodwind, brass and timpani. The adagio lasts for fifteen bars. The sixteenth bar is already the introduction to the allegro where Mozart, whether intentionally or subcon-

sciously introduces a lively theme which is almost identical to one used by his great rival Clementi in his B-flat Sonata, Op. 43, No. 2. Mozart certainly knew the work and Clementi later pointed out Mozart's plagiarism in a roundabout way by emphasizing in reprints that it was played before the Emperor (and Mozart) in 1781. It is an attractive and airy theme which Mozart also echoes in the *Prague* symphony of 1786. But why Mozart should need to use it (unless he was paying Clementi a brotherly compliment) has never been made clear. It suits the purpose admirably in setting the mood of what we might call the Papageno side of the opera. It is given lively quasi-fugal treatment and is soon taken over by the flute, though perhaps with not deliberate significance. The woodwind introduce a new idea while the strings keep dragging back the old theme till the overture comes to a sudden halt at its halfway mark, on the

ABOVE: *Papageno's song,* 'Der Vogelfänger bin ich ja', *from Mozart's original score*

73

dominant B-flat. Marked adagio, the initiate's knocks on the door now come with dramatic effect. Three groups of three chords based on B-flat, identical except for the symbolic over-riding flute. The allegro theme is taken up again, interrupted by the trombones playing firstly soft octaves and then loud groups of five notes aided by the other brass. Having almost moved into G minor there is a silent bar and then the overture gallops away again with strings sticking to their favourite theme, the woodwind answering, the brass commenting. There is a strange *ff* bar moving through D-flat, and B-natural to C, which might be interpreted as a threat, before the overture moves to a typical joyful Mozartian ending. It is a splendid piece of music, but, remembering that it was written in remarkable haste, there seems no point in loading it with too much significance. It is, as Newman says, 'a fascinating blend of sonata and fugue', which Mozart might have conceived for any occasion.

The Introduction to Act I is breathless and full of tremolos and crescendos as Tamino cries out that the serpent is drawing near; the orchestra foreshadowing the 'danger' music later used in silent movies. The melodic line descends as he falls to the ground. The trio of Ladies express first their triumph and then admiration for the fallen youth in a melodious Italianate opera vein which must have forewarned Schikaneder's regulars that they were not in for the usual musical farce. They were no doubt relieved to hear Papageno's merry trills and his delightful song in popular strophic vein of a distinctly Viennese flavour. The third verse was added after the first production. Schikaneder complained to Mozart that he had so much to sing that he had no room to add the traditional topical gags. Today's audiences would probably be very surprised at what went on in Viennese productions of the time and they have no cause to complain when Papageno is played in a true spirit of broad comedy. The simple little five-note phrase of Papageno's flute will play an important part later on.

Tamino's aria as he gazes at Pamina's portrait (*Dies Bildnis*) is, surprisingly, his only solo aria in the whole opera, and its exultant opening phrase is only heard once. Here we are with Mozart at his most exquisite and moving, an immaculately constructed song of poise and polish yet so attentive to the meaning of the words and the emotion in Tamino's breast that it seems full of warmth and truth. There is a lovely scoring at the end for woodwind and horns.

It must be repeated that the Queen of the Night's aria is a piece of operatic deception, musically as well as dramatically. From its duly regal introduction, through its deeply touching first section to its brilliantly pleading and highly virtuosic second part, it suggests no evil. It has true touches of pathos and a nice flare of anger as she mentions the scoundrel (Bösewicht). It is no use forewarned commentators trying to convince us that she is wicked. Only by looking ahead could Newman really justify his nicely turned description 'a vulture with the voice of a nightingale'. Any romantic heroine in a bel canto *opera seria* would have been grateful for this aria. At least Tamino is completely won over—which is surely the point of the aria; and we should be too if we didn't already know the lady's true nature.

As Tamino is about to part on his mission, Papageno, still

dolefully padlocked, tries to talk to Tamino. His melody, faintly echoing the Clementi tune of the overture, is pure Mozart parodying himself with his favourite interval of a descending sixth which he effectively uses to excess in all kinds of music. The whole Quintet, with the Three Ladies joining in its moral message that the world would be a better place if all liars had their lips padlocked, is an effective contrast of very simple harmony with briefly elaborated moments when an important point is to be made. We must not miss the phrase that accompanies the presentation of the vital magic flute, which is heard again at the end of the quintet. Mozart does nothing so obvious as using a flute to portray this moment; he leaves it out altogether. Similarly when Papageno is given his set of bells we are not allowed to hear them right away. This is a well-considered piece of forbearance which pays off later when the magic tones are heard for the first time. But the phrase heard behind the farewell '*lebt wohl*' will be heard again at an effective moment in Act II. At mention of the magic boys the music takes on a special mystical quality which Mozart achieves in various ways each time they appear. The scene ends on a pleasantly happy note with little hint of the solemnity and trials to come. However this came about, it is dramatically right and effective.

BELOW AND OPPOSITE: *Monostatos and Pamina: costume designs by Heinrich Stürmer for Schinkel's Berlin production of 1816*

In the original libretto the second scene opened with three slaves commenting on the hidden action in Sarastro's palace so far, but in performance the dialogue is often omitted and the scene opens in the palace with Monostatos. The accompanying music, as Monostatos threatens Pamina, is not so dramatic or threatening as we might expect; it has an opening tremolo and a very faint 'turkish' flavour with effective woodwind; we are still in the comedy section and Monostatos is still not painted as a truly 'black' villain. Papageno now enters (in most productions with the portrait of Pamina in his possession) describing the fair lady he seeks with music appropriately Papageno-ish. In the brief encounter with Monostatos, Mozart catches perfectly the comic bluff that sums up the cowardly reactions of each with brief nervous but basically light-hearted phrases. The whole trio is in the bright key of G.

With the natural art of someone who understands theatre, Mozart now introduces the delightful '*Bei Männern*' duet which so effectively won the hearts of the audience and has done ever since. Back in the warm key of E-flat, Mozart contrives one of those delicately posed, essentially simple duets (as in the exquisite and ever-popular '*Là ci darem la mano*' in *Don Giovanni*), its poignancy in no way lessened by the fact that the participants are not in love with each other but expressing separate and divergent emotions. It has gently flowing lines that merge but leave each singer's thoughts clearly apart. Mozart discreetly decorates the second verse with woodwind and horns and gently increases the warmth of their passion.

The finale of the first Act is a dramatic portent of the deeper matters to come; the high seriousness begins to creep in with the solemn exhortations of the Three Boys as they lead Tamino to the temples. Mozart prepares us with a lovely orchestral blend that must have sounded quite novel in its time. Ideally it is sung by boys (rather than by female sopranos as in many productions) to lend the right quality of solemn innocence to what is almost an earnest plea, rather than a command, to be 'steadfast, obedient and silent'. Tamino, left alone (music in the simple key of C to a sparse accompaniment) muses on the meaning of the temples he sees. Now Mozart's dramatic writing is heard at its best and a positive rash of accidentals appears in the score as Tamino's determined boldness is gradually undermined at each temple, first in D-minor, then in G-minor, finally in the important C-minor which slides in to A-flat as the Priest, in noble bass tones, comes out to question him. Throughout the questioning Mozart obdurately keeps his key signature in C-minor or A-minor although most of it is, in fact, in diverging keys such as E-flat. The important magic flute obbligato at last comes into play as Tamino expresses his gratitude to the gods, now firmly in C, so ideally suited to the simple enchantment of the animals who come out at the instrument's call. Slightly despairing he plays a scale in G which is exactly answered by the distinctive and now familiar phrase of Papageno's pipes. For a moment there is drama again as Papageno and Pamina enter (as Tamino leaves to look for them). Effectively Mozart contrasts the jerky music of Monostatos who intercepts them with his slaves with the once more eminently Viennese and entrancing music as Papageno remembers his magic bells and plays a melody that sets the villains dancing away out of sight. Yet again Papageno and Pamina take up their sympathetic acquaintance in a charming little duet based on a folksong that also struck a chord in

Schubert's mind some years later. They wish that everyone had such a set of bells so that everyone could live in harmony and friendship. There is a brief fanfare for trumpets and timpani and an offstage chorus is heard praising Sarastro. Papageno (on a flattened A, *à la* Gershwin) wishes he was a mouse; in contrast to which Pamina's affirmation that it is best to tell the truth, even though the telling might be a crime, is a bold phrase on the dominant, then the tonic, that leads powerfully into the first all-out combination of representatives of woodwind, brass and strings in the opera. It is an impressive moment as the Priests and followers salute Sarastro. It was intended in the original that Sarastro would now enter in a triumphal car drawn by three groups of three lions—but this is not eminently practical on the normal operatic stage. Pamina throws herself at his feet to beg forgiveness supported by an anxious repeated figure in the strings, and Sarastro forgives in a wonderfully grave and tender

BELOW: *Costumes for the Queen of the Night, Tamino and Pamina designed by Caramba for a 1923 La Scala production conducted by Toscanini*

LEFT: *A production at the Metropolitan Opera for the 1912–13 season with Edward Lankow as Sarastro*

melody that any bass would delight to sing. The rich plunges of a true basso voice are always a pleasure at this point. Tamino is dragged in by Monostatos to an agitated accompaniment on the violins, and the joy of the lovers is beautifully caught in simple but lyrically placed arpeggios. Monostatos' backing motive is again heard in almost 'Turkish' vein as he reminds Sarastro of his loyalty, but Sarastro condemns him to a flogging. The final chorus is not at all typical Mozart but as four-square as Beethoven might have made it with the whole orchestra for the first time in full voice.

79

ABOVE: *Metropolitan Opera production with Anna Moffo (Pamina), Paul Franke (Monostatos) and Nicolai Gedda (Tamino)*

The March of the Priests that opens Act II is of a totally different kind of solemnity, and for the first time we have a taste of Mozart's masonic style—solemnity tinged with humanity. Sarastro's aria, 'O Isis und Osiris' continues the masonic vein, and the strong orchestration, with three trombones prominent, is pregnant with significance. Only violas and cellos are employed in the strings which gives a profound quality and depth to the sound, making this one of the most solemn moments in the opera so far. In musical terms we are more than halfway through the score at this point. One of the pleasures of *The Magic Flute*'s score is that there is little tedium. Very few moments out-stay their welcome—indeed quite the opposite, as one subtle touch follows another, and there are lovely themes thrown in for brief moments with a profligacy that only a composer of Mozart's fertility could afford. The Ladies prove themselves not unlikeable creatures as they chatter in housewifely fashion and warn Papageno that all is lost as far as he is concerned. Their music combines with Papageno's and Tamino's in a lively section in chirpy quavers. This is dramatically interrupted by the priests off-stage who tell the Ladies to be gone in the usual stern C-minor and frighten them off with a powerful chord accompanied by two loud bursts of thunder. Three chords now accompany the news that the initiates have passed their first test. Monostatos, whom we are beginning to feel is hard done by, is unexpectedly given a rather pleasant, almost jolly, aria as he gazes on the sleeping Pamina. To the accompaniment of piccolo, flute, clarinets and bassoons, with strings, it is intended to have a distant, ethereal quality.

The following aria of the Queen of the Night, 'Der Hölle Rache', is one that is frequently misdirected and misunderstood. Generations of sopranos have treated it as a bel canto exercise for their special benefit and have inclined to make it sound charming. It should be treated (as it rightly is in the Solti recording) as strong and venomous; the repeated notes should be punched home with dagger-like effect—for a dagger is to materialize from them. Mozart's accompaniment is far from pretty; as tempestuous as any yet provided. In direct contrast Sarastro in his subsequent aria, 'In diesen heiligen Hallen', explaining that he and his followers are not vengeful, has a richly charitable theme heard in the rare key, for Mozart, of E-major. It is warmly accompanied by strings with a slight touch of colouring from the flute. In the next scene when the Three Boys appear with the flute and bells and a square meal, Mozart has yet another totally different and, as usual, unique sound to offer. After four atmospheric bars, in 'Seid uns zum zweiten Mal willkommen' the boys' voices float in close harmony above a fairy-like background of tripping strings. The contrasts continue as if Mozart is showing us just how much dramatic variety he can achieve. To the gentle chords and woodwind phrases so beloved of Italian opera composers he gives Pamina a tender, moving aria ('Ach ich fühl's') that he rarely equalled, basically in G-minor, an intimate key, with occasional dramatic ventures in B-flat major. The four square hymn of the Priests is an ideal passage between the preceding tenderness and the emotive quality of the following section where equally tender farewells are taken to sombre but rhythmical accompaniment. At which stage we are greatly relieved and delighted to have yet another of Papageno's hit songs, the ever-popular 'Ein Mädchen oder Weibchen', which has the timeless qualities of a folk-song. It is entirely simple with a most effective touch from the glockenspiel's intimate part in the accompaniment.

ABOVE: *Illustration of an 1865 Paris production at the Théâtre-Lyrique*

The profound finale of *The Magic Flute* is almost a musical resumé of the opera, a succession of balanced movements that round off everything in a dramatically satisfying manner. There is no further dialogue. Starting with the Three Boys, this time radiant in their praise of the Sun, Mozart is now in his most masonic vein, almost Handelian in its rigidity and three-part writing. The first statement of the tune is given to the wind who alternate with strings in the subsequent accompaniment. The placid E-flat of the opening turns to a foreboding C-minor as Pamina is seen with a dagger in her hand. Future composers' 'mad scenes' are anticipated with wonderfully dramatic effect, as Pamina sings of her despair, addressing the dagger as her lover. Strange chromatic touches to the dominating G-minor lead to a dramatic climax against an agitated accompaniment as she raises the dagger to kill herself and is restrained by the Boys. They re-assure her in the confident E-flat of their opening that Tamino still loves her and there is a glowing radiance to their '*Zwei Herzen*' passage proclaiming that true love is guarded by the gods.

OPPOSITE: *Erich Kunz sings Papageno with Irmgard Seefried as Pamina, in Vienna*

ABOVE: *Lucia Popp (Pamina), Werner Hollweg (Tamino) and Hildegard Uhrmacher (Queen of the Night) in a visiting production by the Hamburg Opera at the* Teatro Comunale, *Florence, 1974*

As the scene dramatically changes to the mountains of water and fire with their glowing red background, the music takes on a remarkable sound, with the trombones again lending their dramatic effect. There follows a solemn, relentless fugato for strings, and the Two Men in Armour, one a bass and one a tenor singing an octave higher throughout, read the inscription in 'transparent writing inscribed on a pyramid' to the tune of the old chorale '*Ach Gott von Himmel sieh darein*' which Mozart modifies to his own requirements at the end. The orchestration here produces a strange effect not heard before in Mozart's music as the voice parts are copied by flute, oboe, bassoon and trombones in well-spread octaves and the strings continue their fugato. As Tamino moves to his ordeal, Pamina's voice is heard and Tamino is told that his vow of silence is now over. Pamina has proved herself worthy and is admitted. The lovers embrace and they sing the superbly calm and deeply moving duet that begins with Pamina's '*Tamino mein*', on Mozart's always effectively employed rise of a sixth, in the key of F. Encouraged by the Men in Armour, they now walk toward the mountains, against a musical background suggesting fire, wind, thunder and rushing water. Tamino (reminded by Pamina) bravely plays his flute over the subdued drums and chords of the brass instruments. It is a remarkably tense, concentrated passage. The ordeal by fire over, there is a calm moment as they face the next. Again Tamino's flute is heard in the same strain as they face the ordeal by water. After this the interior of a brightly lit temple is seen and the triumphant lovers are bidden to enter to a blaze of trumpets and drums and a choral welcome.

Papageno's familiar flourish on the pipes is heard as he enters to hang himself. The touch of optimism and low comedy is not lost in the musical accompaniment, setting a mood which encourages most Papagenos to play this scene in a farcical spirit. Indeed, it is an essential foil against which the high moral drama of the rest needs to be set. As Papageno is about to hang himself the Three Boys again intervene and remind him of his magical bells. He takes them out and plays them 'chiming sweet and clearly' in a sweetly innocent and charming tune. The Boys bring in Papagena and there follows one of the most delightful and moving love duets in a vein of lightness and joy that has rarely been equalled in operatic music. It is sheer *opera buffa*, the patter song convention employed in a profoundly moving and satisfying way. Papageno and Papagena have won their happiness, even if in an unheroic manner, and we rejoice with them. They depart to a light-hearted tune; and we see them no more.

In dark contrast, the happy G-major is deserted for the basic drama of the E-flat and C-minor tonalities. Now all is muffled thunder with a strange persistent figure in the strings which has an air of finality about it. The Queen of the Night, the Three Ladies and Monostatos breathe their last moments of defiance before they sink into their own world of 'eternal night'. The final scene is a blaze of sun, visibly and musically. Sarastro, triumphantly aloft with Tamino and Pamina, the Priests and the Three Boys, proclaim the triumph of truth and goodness in a simple, moving, yet radiant way and Mozart offers music of a simple, matter-of-fact nature.

While many people have been worried about the incon-sistencies of character in this opera, the ambiguous nature of the elements that originally stemmed from the Queen of the Night (the Three Boys, the magic flute itself, which, without much explanation end up on Sarastro's side) and the bold contrast of comedy and grandeur—all these things can be comfortably forgotten in the joyful rightness of the music that props up the strange, stagey, fantasy world of the libretto. Operatic history has many worse and far more confusing and irrational plots to offer than this. At least, in *The Magic Flute*, we know what is happening even if we don't always know why. There are many operas where even a careful synopsis still leaves us in a state of bewilderment.

While the text of the opera by Schikaneder, and whoever may have collaborated with him, is never more than adequately literate, the score that Mozart wrote is on a Shakespearean level of inspiration. It has clothed the work in immortality; made it a classic that speaks effectively to every succeeding generation. It bears out Beecham's heartfelt contention that nineteenth-century musicians and commentators were altogether wrong to see Mozart as a slight and charming composer and nothing more; that he was, in fact, a great composer in every sense and that his works deserved to be interpreted with every ounce of dramatic sensibility. There is plenty of lightness and charm in the opera, but there is also a dramatic power that has rarely been surpassed. Above all there is the warmth of humanity which Mozart so adroitly combined with the rightness that led him to be labelled 'classical' in a sense that wrongly implied a finnicky sort of neatness. Mozart took the musical language of his day and glorified it, as Shakespeare did the English language, with phrases of unforgettable clarity and insight.

The supreme test of a musical masterpiece, and one which the academic commentators sometimes forget, is that it is never boring or in any way superfluous in its statement. Of all Mozart's attributes, the greatest is that he never went on too long, always leaving us wishing for more, and what he said was always interesting. The score of *The Magic Flute* is quite simply inspired from beginning to end so that even the most improbable situations are made effective. It stands, with *The Marriage of Figaro*, as one of the great peaks of operatic achievement, its strange story made meaningful by Mozart's strength of purpose and honesty. Not the least of its achievements is the real, warm, unforgettable character of Papageno, the 'Figaro' of the opera, who surely is a reflection of Mozart himself; humble, perhaps misguided in the harsh complexities of life and its demands, but immortal in the magic of the music that he created.

A Survey of Performances and Recordings

The first performance of *The Magic Flute* was on September 30, 1791. Mozart conducted from the keyboard with Susmayr turning the pages for him. The opera had its second performance on October 1 with Mozart again directing. Subsequent performances after October 1 were conducted by J. B. Henneberg, the regular musical director of the theatre. As far as Mozart was concerned it was an enjoyable and satisfying production with most of the cast made up of old acquaintances and friends. Schikaneder, of course, was Papageno and his older brother Urban was the First Priest. Sarastro was sung by Franz Xaver Gerl, the regular bass with the company (for whom Mozart also composed the concert-aria *'Per questa bella mano'*, K612), and his wife Barbara sang Papagena. There were vague rumours that she and Mozart had a brief 'affair' at one time. Mozart's sister-in-law Josepha Hofer, the company's leading soprano, sang the Queen of the Night. Benedikt Schlack, an accomplished musician who played the flute himself for the role, was Tamino, and his wife was also in the cast. They were close friends of the Mozarts. Pamina was sung by Anna Gottlieb who had sung Barbarina in *The Marriage of Figaro* at the age of twelve. The scenery and costumes by Joseph Gayl and Herr Nesthaler were most favourably commented on.

It was reported that the opera was rather coolly received at the beginning but the duet *'Bei Mannern'* pleased the audience and at this point they began to warm to the piece a little. Early audiences were obviously as puzzled by the opera as many later acquaintances have been. Mozart was distressed by the half-hearted applause at the end and had to be dragged onto the stage by Schikaneder to take a curtain-call. The opera was to be repeated some twenty times in October; an unusual run for this company, and by October 7 Mozart was able to report to Constanze, who had returned from Baden-bei-Wien, that the houses were now full and that *'Bei Mannern'* and Papageno's

ABOVE LEFT: *Anna Gottlieb (1774–1856), the first Pamina*

ABOVE RIGHT: *Josepha Hofer (1758–1809), Mozart's sister-in-law and creator of the role of Queen of the Night*

bell-playing were regularly encored. It was, as Mozart said, 'catching on'. On October 8 Mozart was again there and was greatly annoyed by a stupid Bavarian acquaintance who laughed and applauded even in the serious moments. So he left the box and went backstage to play the glockenspiel to which Papageno mimed. He tried to throw Schikaneder by playing when he wasn't and vice versa till Schikaneder amused everyone by telling him to shut up. It was the first time the audience had realised that Schikaneder was not actually playing the bells. Mozart took his mother-in-law along on the next night and again on October 13 when Antonio Salieri and his mistress joined them and Salieri greatly pleased Mozart by his praise, saying that it was fit to be performed before the greatest of kings on the greatest of occasions. He promised to come again many times.

The Magic Flute now became a popular entertainment and people were having to arrive three hours early in order to get a seat. It is said that Mozart received 100 ducats for his score. Some of the music was published on November 5. It has also been remarked that Schikaneder dealt unfairly with Mozart when he was alive and failed to pay his family anything after his death for the work's continued performances. There had been 223 performances at his theatre by May 1851, and credit must fairly be given for the way he built *The Magic Flute* into a success. By the time the Theater an der Wien was built a statue of Papageno was included in the decorations.

No journalistic report of the first night has survived but the correspondent of the Berlin *Musikalisches Wochenblatt* who had been there on October 9 wrote that the opera 'given at great cost and with much magnificence in the scenery, fails to have the hoped-for success, the contents and language of the piece being altogether too bad'. He looked forward to the arrival of Cimarosa with some new works. This is somewhat at odds with Mozart's own views and other general evidence of its growing popularity.

Mozart had intended to take Constanze again on October 15 but was unwell. By November 20 he was mortally sick and never left his bed again. As he declined he was constantly imagining what they would be doing on the stage at that moment and wishing he could hear his music just once again. He died on December 5, 1791. The final mystery of his life was why his masonic friends allowed him to be buried in an unmarked grave. It has been explained that funerals were not generally elaborate at this time; that Mozart's was not, as often said, a pauper's funeral, but simply the cheapest possible.

Soon after his death, Mozart and his music began to arouse increasingly favourable comments; so many, in fact, that there was even a strong reaction in places. *The Magic Flute*, which had itself come in on a fashion for 'magic' operas, was the inspirer of many others and, moreover, the inspiration of much that was to happen in the shaping of romantic opera to come. Its advanced musical ideas alone were a source of ideas for many subsequent composers. It took some time to obtain a pension for Mozart's widow, but in the meantime several benefit performances were given on her behalf including a special performance of *The Magic Flute* organized by Schikaneder.

OPPOSITE: *Two early productions: (above) Berlin, 1911; (below) Glyndebourne Festival Opera 1935 with Edwin Ziegler as Monostatos, Aulikki Rautawaara as Pamina and Walther Ludwig as Tamino*

His operas continued to flourish. *The Magic Flute* itself was performed in Prague in October 1792 and again in 1794 in both Italian and Czech. It was heard in Germany by 1793 but not in Berlin until 1794. It was greatly admired by Goethe who heard it at Weimar in 1794 with German words supplied by his brother-in-law C. A. Vulpius. Goethe began to write a sequel to it but abandoned the project. In Beethoven's sketchbooks for *Fidelio* several quotes from *The Magic Flute* are to be found.

For a Paris performance in 1801 the libretto was entirely re-written. The opera did not reach England until 1811 when it was correctly performed at the Haymarket Theatre in German; and it was heard in the original language at Covent Garden in 1833. George Hogarth in his *Memoirs of the Musical Drama* written in 1838 was already expressing the bewilderment of most commentators, finding it of 'that mystical stamp which is congenial to the German mind' but which rendered it 'nearly unintelligible' elsewhere. 'Well calculated to excite the German imagination, he continues but 'it must ever be a cause of regret that his [Mozart's] most enchanting strains should not have been called forth by a subject more fitted to rouse the feelings and sympathies of our nature.' Its dramatic defects were felt everywhere but in Germany; the Italians reducing it to 'a childish and insipid fairy tale'. It had been heard in England 'never with much effect', he reported, until it was done in English at Drury Lane 'last season', when 'notwithstanding the heaviness of the piece, the music (which was well performed) was found so charming, that it sustained a considerable number of representations'. The opera remained almost unknown but, writes Hogarth, its 'airs became generally familiar—some of them as much so as the most popular English ballads. And not only its airs, but its concerted pieces and choruses, are the delight of every one who gets enjoyment from the cultivation of music. *The Magic Flute* illustrates the close alliance between the utmost simplicity and the highest beauties of the art. When this opera was first produced, its melodies were instantly heard in every dwelling, from palace to cottage; they resounded in the streets, the highways and the fields; and it was truly said that Mozart had enchanted all Germany with his Enchanted Flute. The beauties are not of that recondite kind which are perceptible only to the practised ear and cultivated taste of the musician; they delight equally the learned and the

RIGHT: *Covent Garden, 1931, with Margarete Teschemacher as Pamina and Gerhard Hüsch as Papageno*

unlearned. And the spinners and knitters in the sun, will listen to them with as heartfelt pleasure as the most refined frequenters of our theatres and concert-rooms. They reach the heart at once and the impression remains for ever.'

Despite this, the opera was not much heard until it was revived in 1911 by the Cambridge University Music Society in the excellent translation by Professor Dent. But it was largely the championship of Sir Thomas Beecham that brought it back into favour with his production in 1914 at Drury Lane. It was in the regular repertoire of the Old Vic and Sadler's Wells from 1921, was first performed at Glyndebourne in 1935 under Fritz Busch, revived at Salzburg in 1937 under Toscanini, at Covent Garden in 1938 again under Beecham, at Salzburg again under Furtwängler in 1949. Nowadays one has to book several months ahead even to get a seat and the opera continues to be the subject of keen appraisal and much enjoyment. The recent

ABOVE: *Christa Ludwig, Elisabeth Schwarzkopf and Martha Hoffgen as the Three Ladies in a 1964 recording of* The Magic Flute

LEFT: *Pilar Lorengar rehearsing for the role of Pamina*

93

Glyndebourne performance added highly imaginative decor by a celebrated modern artist and its Papageno could hardly have been played with greater gusto by Schikaneder himself than it was by Benjamin Luxon.

Still, perhaps, one hopes that the cinema or television might really take the plunge and, rather than filming a stage production, will one day give us a *Magic Flute* that is as full of science fiction marvels as its creators first imagined. It would be exciting to see the mountains really split asunder.

There are many people today, in a modern echo of Hogarth's sentiments, who enjoy the opera on record and, although it is always difficult to admit, revel in its music without worrying too much about its plot. Certainly they have been well served. The first complete recording was made in 1937, aptly enough under the direction of Sir Thomas Beecham (World

LEFT: *Richard Tauber, a famous Tamino*

Records SH158/60). The recording is still with us and greatly treasured not least for the vivacious orchestral contribution that Beecham provides. Certainly the Papageno portions have rarely been done with more gusto and there are delightful performances from Tiana Lemnitz as Pamina and Gerhard Hüsch as Papageno. Least attractive is what has been described as the 'violent Heldentenor style' of Roswaenge as Tamino and a roguish Sarastro. The monaural sound is still quite acceptable.

We are also well-served by the other recordings currently available. Of the older ones, the 1955 version under Böhm is now on a cheap label (Decca GOS501/3) and presents a warm, friendly, firmly conducted performance with Hilde Gueden at her best as Pamina; while the 1956 recording under Fricsay is almost as lively as Beecham's, handles the mysterious parts well and has an excellent Papageno in Dietrich Fischer-Dieskau. It

RIGHT: *Dietrich Fischer-Dieskau, who recorded the role of Papageno twice*

has the essential dialogue and is on a bargain label (Heliodor 2701 015). Karajan's 1952 recording (HMV SLS5052) has a distinguished cast with Seefried excellent as Pamina and Erich Kunz a lively Papageno. The Three Boys are not too satisfactory and Karajan is occasionally inclined to rush the singers.

Of the recordings made in the 1960s, Klemperer's 1964 performance (HMV SLS912) is a curious mixture of grandeur and complacency. He naturally savours the heavier parts and gives the work great stature, but he also highlights the humour. It is an impressive performance, yet perhaps lacking in overall dramatic tension. The orchestral playing is excellent. Nicolai Gedda makes an ideal manly, yet lyrical Tamino, and Gundula Janowitz is a gentle and melancholic Pamina. In keeping with Klemperer's weighty approach he has a less frivolous Papageno than some in Walter Berry who nevertheless handles the lightly romantic parts well, and Gottlob Frick is an impressively stern Sarastro. Lucia Popp is a steely Queen of the Night. A special minor delight is to be found in the singing of Ludwig and Schwarzkopf as two of the three Ladies. Dialogue is not included.

OPPOSITE: *Joan Sutherland as Queen of the Night at Covent Garden in 1962*

Böhm's 1965 recording (DG 2709 017) is beautifully balanced and is one of the most satisfying views of the score. Full of precision and grace, light and lyrical, with classic performances to be savoured from Fritz Wunderlich as a glowing Tamino and Dietrich Fischer-Dieskau as a comic and ebullient Papageno. The female roles are less satisfactory.

Perhaps the liveliest version on disc is that conducted by Georg Solti (Decca SET479/81) who keeps his natural forcefulness under control and leads the Vienna Philharmonic in a radiant performance with the ensembles in perfect accord. Stuart Burrows makes a fine, manly Tamino, and Hermann Prey is a lightly roguish Papageno. Martti Talvela is one of the finest Sarastros, and Pilar Lorengar is a glowing Pamina. To find Fischer-Dieskau in the minor role of The Speaker is to put the strength of this cast in perspective. A performance in Swedish is taken from a film soundtrack and serves simply as a memento of Ingmar Bergman's production.

A perfect *Magic Flute* seems almost beyond expectation. To recommend one of these recordings above any other is not easy. Solti has the best overall cast, but some reviewers find him lacking in the charm that Böhm so naturally achieves. Böhm's recording is probably the best in orchestral terms and notable for the inclusion of the late Fritz Wunderlich but is weak on the feminine side. Choice probably lies between these two depending on whether you want an exuberant or a graceful reading. The Klemperer presents a noble view of the work; while few Mozartians would wish to be without Beecham's very personal and historical recording. A satisfactory taste of the opera could be had from any of the older and cheaper versions. Highlights from some of these recordings are available. Above all, let us be grateful for the technical magic that we all have at our fingertips today, that allows us, whenever we feel inclined, to enter the strange, wonderful, intriguing, puzzling but, above all enchanting world of Mozart's *Magic Flute*.

Libretto

English translation by Charles Osborne

NOTE: Following standard theatre practice the dialogue has been abridged and therefore may vary slightly in detail from the author's synopsis.

ERSTER AKT

(Rauhe Felsengegend. Tamino eilt herbei. Eine Schlange verfolgt ihn.)

TAMINO

Zu Hilfe! zu Hilfe! Sonst bin ich verloren,
Der listigen Schlange zum Opfer erkoren!
Barmherzige Götter! Schon nahet sie sich!
Ach rettet mich! ach schützet mich!

(Er sinkt erschöpft und bewusstlos zusammen. Die drei Damen, mit silbernen Wurfspiessen, ireten ein. Sie durchbohren mit ihren Wurfspiessen die Schlange.)

DIE DREI DAMEN

Stirb, Ungeheu'r, durch uns're Macht!
Triumph! Triumph! Sie ist vollbracht,
Die Heldenthat! Er ist befreit
Durch unsers Armes Tapferkeit.

ERSTE DAME

Ein holder Jüngling, sanft und schön!

ZWEITE DAME

So schön, als ich noch nie geseh'n!

DRITTE DAME

Ja, ja, gewiss zum Malen schön!

DIE DAMEN

Würd' ich mein Herz der Liebe weih'n.
So müsst es dieser Jüngling sein.
Lasst uns zu uns'rer Fürstin eilen,
Ihr diese Nachricht zu erteilen.
Vielleicht, dass dieser schöne Mann
Die vor'ge Ruhe ihr geben kann.

ACT I

(A rocky desert. Tamino enters, pursued by a serpent.)

TAMINO

Help, rescue me or I am lost. The cunning serpent has overpowered me. Merciful Gods, it draws nearer. Save me, protect me.

(He faints. Three Ladies carrying spears appear and kill the serpent.)

LADIES

Die, monster, by our power. Victory is ours, the heroic deed is accomplished. Our valour has saved him.

FIRST LADY

A lovely youth, gentle and handsome.

SECOND LADY

A more handsome creature I have never seen.

THIRD LADY

Yes, indeed, fit to be painted.

LADIES

If I were to allow my heart to love, it would be this youth. Let us hasten to our Sovereign with this news. Perhaps this handsome man can bring repose to her again.

ERSTE DAME

So geht und sagt es ihr,
Ich bleib' indessen hier.

ZWEITE DAME

Nein, nein, geht ihr nur hin,
Ich wache hier für ihn!

DRITTE DAME

Nein, nein, das kann nicht sein,
Ich schütze ihn allein.

ERSTE DAME

Ich bleib' indessen hier!

ZWEITE DAME

Ich wache hier für ihn!

DRITTE DAME

Ich schütze ihn allein!

ERSTE DAME

Ich bleibe!

ZWEITE DAME

Ich wache!

DRITTE DAME

Ich schütze!

DIE DAMEN

Ich! ich! ich!
Ich sollte fort? Ei, ei! Wie fein!
Sie wären gern bei ihm allein.
Nein, nein, das kann nicht sein.
Was wollte ich darum nicht geben,
Könnt' ich mit diesem Jüngling leben!
Hätt' ich ihn doch so ganz allein!
Doch keine geht, es kann nicht sein.
Am besten ist es nun, ich geh'.—
Du Jüngling, schön und liebevoll!
Du trauter Jüngling, lebe wohl,
Bis ich dich wieder seh'.

FIRST LADY

Go, then, and tell her. I'll stay here
meanwhile.

SECOND LADY

No, no, you go. I shall watch over him.

THIRD LADY

No, I can't have that. I alone shall
protect him.

FIRST LADY

I'll stay here meanwhile.

SECOND LADY

I shall watch over him.

THIRD LADY

I alone shall protect him.

FIRST LADY

I shall stay.

SECOND LADY

I shall guard.

THIRD LADY

I shall protect.

LADIES

I! I! I! Must I go? Oh no. How subtle
they are. They each want to stay alone
with him. No, no, that can't be. What
wouldn't I give to live with this youth
alone. If I could get him by myself. But
neither of them will go, it's no use. I'd
better be off. I'm going. Goodbye, you
fair and lovely youth, until I see you
again.

(*Sie entfernen sich.*) (*Papageno, auf dem Rücken einen grossen Vogelbauer erhebend, eilt herbei.*)

PAPAGENO

Der Vogelfänger bin ich ja,
Stets lustig, heisa, hopsasa!
Der Vogelfänger ist bekannt
Bei Alt und Jung im ganzen Land.
Weiss mit dem Locken umzugehn
Und mich auf's Pfeifen zu verstehn.
Drum kann ich froh und lustig sein
Denn alle Vögel sind ja mein.
Der Vogelfänger bin ich ja,
Stets lustig, heisa, hopsasa!
Der Vogelfänger ist bekannt
Bei Alt und Jung im ganzen Land.
Ein Netz für Mädchen möchte ich,
Ich fing sie dutzendweis für mich;
Dann sperrte ich sie bei mir ein,
Und alle Mädchen wären mein.
Wenn alle Mädchen wären mein,
Dann tauschte ich brav Zucker ein,
Die, welche mir am liebsten wär',
Der gäb' ich gleich den Zucker her.
Und küsste sie mich zärtlich dann,
Wär' sie mein Weib und ich ihr Mann.
Sie schlief an meiner Seite ein,
Ich wiegte wie ein Kind sie ein.

TAMINO
(*er erwacht*)
He da!

PAPAGENO

Was da?

TAMINO

Sag' mir, du lustiger
Freund, wer du bist?

PAPAGENO

Wer ich bin?
Dumme Frage!

(*The ladies depart. Papageno, carrying a cage of birds on his back, enters*).

PAPAGENO

Hey, hey, I'm the birdcatcher. I'm always merry, young and old throughout the land recognise me. I know how to ensnare the birds with my call. I can be happy and light-hearted, because all the birds are mine. I wish I could catch girls as well, I'd like to net them by the dozen. I'd lock them up with me, and they'd all be mine. And if all the girls were mine, then I'd choose the one I liked best to be my wife. she would lie by my side, and I'd cradle her in my arms like a child.

TAMINO

(*Comes to*)
Hey, there.

PAPAGENO

What's that?

TAMINO

Who are you, friend?

PAPAGENO

Who am I? What a silly question, I'm a man like you. What if I should ask who you are?

Ein Mensch wie du.—Wenn ich dich
nun fragte, wer du bist?

TAMINO

Mein Vater ist Fürst, der über viele
Länder und Menschen herrscht; darum
nennt man mich Prinz.

PAPAGENO

Wie er mich so starr anblickt! Bald
fang' ich an, mich vor ihm zu fürchten.
Bleib zurück, sag' ich, und traue mir
nicht, denn ich habe Riesenkraft.

TAMINO

Riesenkraft? Also warst du wohl gar
mein Erretter, der diese giftige Schlange
bekämpfte?

PAPAGENO

Schlange? Was? Wo? Ist sie tot oder
lebendig?

TAMINO

Wie hast du dieses Ungeheuer
bekämpft? Du bist ohne Waffen!

PAPAGENO

Brauch' keine! Bei mir ist ein starker
Druck mit der Hand mehr als Waffen.

TAMINO

Du hast sie also erdrosselt?

PAPAGENO

Erdrosselt!

(Für sich.)

Bin in meinem Leben nicht so stark
gewesen, als heute.

(Die drei Damen erscheinen verschleiert.)

TAMINO

My father is the ruler of many countries
and people, so I am called a prince.

PAPAGENO

How he goes on staring. Why are you
looking at me so suspiciously? I warn
you, keep your distance. If I lay hold of
you, you'll see I have the strength of a
giant.

TAMINO

The strength of a giant? So it was you
who fought this serpent?

PAPAGENO

Serpent? What? Where? Is it dead or
alive?

TAMINO

How did you fight this monster? You
have no weapon.

PAPAGENO

I don't need one. My hands are stronger
than any weapon.

TAMINO

So you strangled it?

PAPAGENO

Strangled?

(Aside:)

I've never been as strong as this before.

(The three ladies enter.)

DIE DAMEN

Papageno!

PAPAGENO

Aha! Das geht mich an.
Sieh dich um, Freund!

TAMINO

Wer sind diese Damen?

PAPAGENO

Wer sie eigentlich sind, weiss ich selbst
nicht.

TAMINO

Sie sind vermutlich sehr schön?

PAPAGENO

Ich denke nicht! Denn wenn sie schön
wären, würden sie ihre Gesichter nicht
bedecken.

DIE DAMEN

Papageno!

PAPAGENO

Hier, meine Schönen, übergeb' ich
meine Vögel.

ERSTE DAME

Dafür schickt dir unsere Fürstin heute
zum erstenmal statt Wein reines, helles
Wasser.

ZWEITE DAME

Und mir befahl sie, dass ich, statt
Zuckerbrot, diesen Stein dir
überbringen soll.

DRITTE DAME

Und statt der süssen Feigen hab' ich die

LADIES

Papageno!

PAPAGENO

Ah, they've come to see me. See these
ladies, my friend?

TAMINO

Who are they?

PAPAGENO

Who they really are I don't know
myself.

TAMINO

Presumably they are very beautiful.

PAPAGENO

I shouldn't think so. If they were
beautiful, they wouldn't hide their faces.

LADIES

Papageno!

PAPAGENO

Here, my lovely ones, here are my
birds.

FIRST LADY

In return for which our Sovereign sends
you for the first time, instead of wine,
pure clear water.

SECOND LADY

And, instead of bread, she gives you
this stone.

THIRD LADY

And, instead of sweet figs, I have the
honour to put on your mouth this
golden lock. It was we who freed you,

Ehre, dir dies goldene Schloss vor den Mund zu legen.
Wir waren's Jüngling, die dich befreiten. Hier, dies Gemälde überschickt dir die grosse Fürstin, es ist das Bildnis ihrer Tochter! Auf Wiedersehen!

TAMINO

Dies Bildnis ist bezaubernd schön,
Wie noch kein Auge je gesehn!
Ich fühl' es, wie dies Götterbild
Mein Herz mit neuer Regung füllt.
Dies Etwas kann ich zwar nicht nennen,
Doch fühl' ich's hier wie Feuer brennen.
Soll die Empfindung Liebe sein?
Ja, ja! die Liebe ist's allein. —
O, wenn ich sie nur finden könnte!
O, wenn sie doch schon vor mir stände!
Ich würde — würde — warm und rein —
Was würde ich? — Ich würde sie voll Entzücken
An diesen heissen Busen drücken,
Und ewig wäre sie dann mein.

(Kurzer, starker Donner.)

TAMINO

Ihr Götter! Was ist das?

DIE DAMEN

Sie kommt!

(Die Berge teilen sich, man erblikt der Königin der Nacht.)

KÖNIGIN

O zitt're nicht, mein lieber Sohn!
Du bist unschuldig, weise, fromm;
Ein Jüngling, so wie du, vermag am besten,
Das tiefbetrübte Mutterherz zu trösten.

Prince. Here, accept this locket which our mighty ruler sends you. It contains the portrait of her daughter. Farewell.

TAMINO

This portrait is bewitchingly beautiful, lovelier than anything that ever was seen before. I feel my heart overflowing with a new kind of feeling. I cannot name this emotion, yet I feel it burning within me like a fire. Can it be love? Yes, it is love alone. Oh, if only I could find her, if she were already standing before me. I would — with pure warmth I would — what would I do? I would hold the charming creature against my aching heart, and she would be mine forever.

(There is a sound of thunder.)

TAMINO

Ye Gods, what was that?

LADIES

She comes.

(The rocks divide, revealing the Queen of the Night.)

QUEEN

Do not be afraid, beloved son. You have innocence, wisdom, holiness. To such a youth as you, a humble mother's heart can turn in trust. All is sorrow to me since I have lost my daughter. My

Zum Leiden bin ich auserkoren,
Denn meine Tochter fehlt mir;
Durch sie ging all mein Glück verloren,
Ein Bösewicht entfloh mit ihr.
Noch seh' ich ihr Zittern
Mit bangem Erschüttern,
Ihr ängstliches Beben,
Ihr schüchternes Streben.
Ich musste sie mir rauben sehen,
Ach helft! war alles, was sie sprach;
Allein vergebens war ihr Flehen,
Denn meine Hilfe war zu schwach.
Du wirst sie zu befreien gehen,
Du wirst der Tochter Retter sein;
Und werd' ich dich als Sieger sehen,
So sei sie dann auf ewig dein.

(Sie tritt zurück. Papageno kommt zurück und zeigt an seinem Mund)

happiness departed with her. A villain abducted her. I still see her trembling and quaking with fear, still see her trying to break free. I saw her being stolen from me. 'Oh help, help,' was all she said. My entreaties were useless, my strength too slight. You, you shall go to rescue her. You shall be my daughter's saviour. And when I see you return victorious, she shall be yours for ever.

(She and the ladies disappear. Papageno returns, pointing to the padlock.)

PAPAGENO

Hm! hm! hm! hm! hm! hm! hm! hm!

PAPAGENO

Hm, hm, hm, hm.

TAMINO

Der Arme kann von Strafe sagen,
Denn seine Sprache ist dahin.

TAMINO

The poor man's lack of voice speaks eloquently of his punishment.

PAPAGENO

Hm! hm! hm! hm! hm! hm! hm! hm!

PAPAGENO

Hm, hm, hm, hm.

TAMINO

Ich kann nichts thun, als dich beklagen,
Weil ich zu schwach zu helfen bin.

TAMINO

Alas, I can do nothing, for I am too weak to be able to help you.

(Die drei Damen erscheinen.)

(The three ladies return.)

ERSTE DAME

(zu Papageno)

Die Königin begnadet dich,
Erlässt die Strafe dir durch mich.

FIRST LADY

(to Papageno)

Our Queen has graciously released you from your punishment.

PAPAGENO

Nun plaudert Papageno wieder.

PAPAGENO

Now Papageno can chatter again.

ZWEITE DAME

Ja, plaud're! Lüge nur nicht wieder.

PAPAGENO

Ich lüge nimmermehr. Nein! Nein!

DRITTE DAME

Dies Schloss soll deine Warnung sein!

PAPAGENO

Dies Schloss soll meine Warnung sein!

ALLE

Bekämen doch die Lügner alle
Ein solches Schloss vor ihren Mund:
Statt Hass, Verleumdung, schwarzer
Galle,
Bestünde Lieb' und Bruderbund.

ERSTE DAME

(übergiebt Tamino die goldene Flöte)

O Prinz, nimm dies Geschenk von mir!
Dies sendet uns're Fürstin dir.
Die Zauberflöte wird dich schützen,
Im grössten Unglück unterstützen.

DIE DAMEN

Hiermit kannst du allmächtig handeln,
Der Menschen Leidenschaft
verwandeln.
Der Traurige wird freudig sein,
Den Hagestolz nimmt Liebe ein.

ALLE

O, so eine Flöte ist mehr als Gold und
Kronen wert,
Denn durch sie wird Menschenglück
und Zufriedenheit vermehrt.

PAPAGENO

Nun, ihr schönen Frauenzimmer,
Darf ich—so empfehl' ich mich.

SECOND LADY

You may chatter, but don't tell lies any
more.

PAPAGENO

No, no, I'll never lie again.

THIRD LADY

This lock should be a warning to you.

PAPAGENO

This lock shall be a warning to me.

ALL

If only all liars' mouths could be locked,
then instead of hatred, slander and
bitterness we would have love and
brotherhood.

FIRST LADY

(giving Tamino a golden flute)

O Prince, accept this gift which our
Queen sends you. This magic flute will
protect and defend you in times of
danger.

LADIES

It will give you great and mysterious
powers. Its notes can turn sorrow to
joy, old bachelors into ardent lovers.

ALL

A flute like this is worth more than gold
and power, for through it mankind can
achieve happiness and harmony.

PAPAGENO

Now, my lovely ladies, may I take my
leave of you?

DIE DAMEN

Dich empfehlen kannst du immer,
Doch bestimmt die Fürstin dich,
Mit dem Prinzen ohn' Verweilen
Nach Sarastros Burg zu eilen.

PAPAGENO

Nein, dafür bedank' ich mich!
Von Euch selber hörte ich,
Dass er wie ein Tigertier!
Sicher liess ohn'alle Gnaden
Mich Sarastro rupfen, braten,
Setzte mich den Hunden für.

DIE DAMEN

Dich schützt der Prinz, trau' ihm allein!
Dafür sollst du sein Diener sein.

PAPAGENO

Dass doch der Prinz beim Teufel wäre!
Mein Leben ist mir lieb;
Am Ende schleicht bei meiner Ehre,
Er von mir wie ein Dieb.

ERSTE DAME

(übergiebt Papageno ein Kästchen mit einem Glockenspiel)

Hier, nimm dies Kleinod, es ist dein.

PAPAGENO

Ei, ei! was mag darinnen sein?

DIE DAMEN

Darinnen hörst du Glöckchen tönen.

PAPAGENO

Werd' ich sie auch wohl spielen
können?

DIE DAMEN

O ganz gewiss! ja, ja, gewiss!

LADIES

You may, but first hear what the Queen
commands. You must hasten without
delay with the Prince to Sarastro's
castle.

PAPAGENO

Oh no, not me. I've heard from you of
his fierceness. If I were to be caught, I'd
be plucked and roasted or thrown to the
dogs.

LADIES

The Prince will protect you. Rely on
him. You shall be his servant.

PAPAGENO

To the devil with the Prince. My life is
dear to me. I'm sure he'd sneak away
from me like a thief when the time
came.

FIRST LADY

(She gives him a chime of bells.)
Here, take this precious gift. It is yours.

PAPAGENO

Hey, I wonder what this is.

LADIES

You'll hear the magic chime of bells.

PAPAGENO

Oh, I'd love to play this.

LADIES

Of course you may.

ALLE

Silberglöckchen, Zauberflöten
Sind zu eurem Schutz vonnöten.
Lebet wohl! wir wollen gehn,
Lebet wohl! auf Wiedersehn.

TAMINO

Doch, schöne Damen, saget an—

PAPAGENO

—Wie man die Burg wohl finden kann?

BEIDE

Wie man die Burg wohl finden kann?

DIE DAMEN

Drei Knäbchen, jung, schön, hold und
weise,
Umschweben euch auf eurer Reise;
Sie werden eure Führer sein,
Folgt ihrem Rate ganz allein.

TAMINO UND PAPAGENO

Drei Knäbchen, jung, schön, hold und
weise,
Umschweben uns auf unsrer Reise.

ALLE

So lebet wohl! wir wollen gehn,
Lebt wohl, lebt wohl! Auf Wiedersehn!

VERWANDLUNG

(Zimmer in Sarastros Palast.)

MONOSTATOS

(Pamina an der Hand hereinschleudernd)
Du feines Täubchen, nur herein!

PAMINA

O welche Marter! Welche Pein!

ALL

Silver bells and magic flute are both for
your protection. Farewell, we must go.

TAMINO

But, beautiful ladies, first tell us—

PAPAGENO

—how to find the way to the castle.

BOTH

Yes, how to find the way to the castle.

LADIES

Three boys, young, fair, kind and wise
will always be near you on your
journey, and will lead you. Follow their
counsel alone.

TAMINO AND PAPAGENO

Three boys, young, fair, kind and wise
will always be near us on our journey.

ALL

Farewell, we must go. Goodbye.

CHANGE OF SCENE

(A room within Sarastro's fortress.)

MONOSTATOS

(Enters, dragging in Pamina.)
Come here, you pretty little dove.

PAMINA

O what torment, what pain.

MONOSTATOS

Verloren ist dein Leben.

PAMINA

Der Tod macht mich nicht beben,
Nur meine Mutter dauert mich;
Sie stirbt vor Gram ganz sicherlich.

MONOSTATOS

He, Sklaven! Legt ihr Fesseln an!
(Sklaven eilen hinzu, um Pamina zu fesseln)
Mein Hass soll dich verderben.

PAMINA

O lass mich lieber sterben,
Weil nichts, Barbar! dich rühren kann.

(Sie sinkt ohnmächtig.)

MONOSTATOS

Nun fort! lasst mich bei ihr allein.

(Sklaven eilen mit den Fesseln durch die
Mitte ab. Papageno erscheint)

PAPAGENO

Wo bin ich wohl? Wo mag ich sein?
Aha, da find' ich Leute!
Gewagt, ich geh' herein.
Schön Mädchen, jung und fein,
Viel weisser noch als Kreide!

(Papageno steht bei Monostatos Anblick
erstarrt; einer erschrickt über den andern.)

BEIDE

Hu! Das ist—der Teu—fel si—cherlich!
Hab' Mitleid—und verschone mich!
Hu! hu! hu!

(Sie laufen, indem sie sich gegenseitig
verstohlen.)

PAMINA
(erwachend)
Mutter! Mutter!

MONOSTATOS

Your life will soon be over.

PAMINA

I'm not afraid of death. But if anything
were to happen to me, my mother
would certainly die of grief.

MONOSTATOS

Hey there, slaves. Bring her chains in.

(Slaves do so.)

Out of hate, I'll compel you to—

PAMINA

Oh, let me die, for nothing will move
you, barbarian.

(She faints.)

MONOSTATOS

Now go, leave her with me alone.

(Slaves depart. Papageno appears.)

PAPAGENO

What is this? Where am I now? Ah,
there are people here. Well, I'll go in.
Lovely maiden, young and fair, your
skin is whiter than chalk.

(He and Monostatos catch sight of each other
simultaneously, and are both terrified.)

BOTH

Ah! It surely must be the devil.
Have mercy.
Spare me.
Oh-h-h.

(They run off in opposite directions.)

PAMINA

(coming to:)

Oh mother, mother!

PAPAGENO

Bin ich nicht ein Narr, dass ich mich schrecken liess? Ach, sieh da! Hier ist das schöne Mädchen noch. Du Tochter der nächtlichen Königin.

PAMINA

O, ich bin es.

PAPAGENO

Das will ich gleich erkennen.

(*Er prüft das Porträt*)

PAMINA

Erlaube mir—
Ja, ich bin's. Wie kam es in deine Hände? ,

PAPAGENO

Ich muss dir das umständlicher erzählen. Ich kam heute früh, wie gewöhnlich, zu deiner Mutter Palast meine Vögel abzugeben, dort sah ich einen Menschen vor mir, der sich Prinz nennen lässt. Dieser Prinz hat deine Mutter so eingenommen, dass sie ihm dein Bildnis schenkte und ihm befahl, dich zu befreien. Sein Entschluss war so schnell, als seine Liebe zu dir.

PAMINA

Liebe? Er liebt mich also?

PAPAGENO

Das glaub' ich dir—Wo blieb ich denn?

PAMINA

Bei der Liebe.

PAPAGENO

Richtig, bei der Liebe. Nun sind wir hier, in den Palast deiner Mutter zu eilen.

PAPAGENO

What an ass I am to get frightened so easily. Ah, here's the beautiful maiden still. Daughter of the mighty ruler of night.

PAMINA

I am she.

PAPAGENO

That I'll soon know.

(*He produces the portrait.*)

PAMINA

Allow me. Yes, this is my likeness. How did you come to have it?

PAPAGENO

I can tell you that easily enough. This morning I went as usual to your mother's palace with a delivery of beautiful birds. Just as I was coming away I met a man who calls himself a prince. Your mother is so fond of him that she gave him your portrait and ordered him to rescue you. Immediately, he resolved to do so and fell in love with you.

PAMINA

In love? Does he really love me?

PAPAGENO

Yes, I believe so. Now what was I saying?

PAMINA

About his being in love.

PAPAGENO

Ah yes, in love. So we came here quickly to carry you off to your mother even more quickly.

PAMINA

Wohl denn, es sei gewagt! Wenn dieser
nun ein böser Geist von Sarastros
Gefolge wäre?

PAPAGENO

Ich ein böser Geist? Wo denkst du him.
Ich bin der beste Geist von der Welt.

PAMINA

Freund, vergieb, vergieb, wenn ich dich
beleidigte. Du hast ein gefühlvolles
Herz.

PAPAGENO

Ach, freilich hab' ich ein gefühlvolles
Herz. Aber wenn ich bedenke, dass
Papageno noch keine Papagena hat!

PAMINA

Armer Mann! Du hast also noch kein
Weib?

PAPAGENO

Noch nicht einmal ein Mädchen, viel
weniger ein Weib!

PAMINA

Bei Männern, welche Liebe fühlen,
Fehlt auch ein gutes Herze nicht.

PAPAGENO

Die süssen Triebe mitzufühlen,
Ist dann der Weiber erste Pflicht.

BEIDE

Wir wollen uns der Liebe freun,
Wir leben durch die Lieb' allein.

PAMINA

Die Lieb' versüsset jede Plage,
Ihr opfert jede Kreatur.

PAMINA

Yes, I'll risk it. But wait, you may be
some evil spirit in Sarastro's employ.

PAPAGENO

Me, evil? I'm the nicest spirit in the
world.

PAMINA

My friend, forgive me if I have made
you sad. You have a tender heart.

PAPAGENO

Well, of course I have a tender heart.
But when I think that Papageno still has
no Papagena!

PAMINA

You poor man, you have no wife?

PAPAGENO

I haven't a sweetheart, let alone a wife.

PAMINA

The heart of him who feels love is
always kind.

PAPAGENO

And woman's first duty is to share this
sweet impulse.

BOTH

We therefore dedicate ourselves to love,
and live for love alone.

PAMINA

Love soothes the wounds that all
creatures feel.

PAPAGENO

Sie würzet uns're Lebenstage,
Sie wirkt im Kreise der Natur.

BEIDE

Ihr hoher Zweck zeigt deutlich an,
Nichts edlers sei, als Weib und Mann.
Mann und Weib, und Weib und Mann,
Reichen an die Gottheit an.

VERWANDLUNG

(Hain, in dessen Mitte drei Tempel. Die
drei Knaben mit silbernen Palmzweigen in
der Hand von links vorn kommend, geleiten
Tamino, der seine Flöte umgehängt trägt.)

DIE DREI KNABEN

Zum Ziele führt dich diese Bahn,
Doch musst du, Jüngling, männlich
siegen.
Drum höre uns're Lehre an:
Sei standhaft, duldsam und
verschwiegen.

TAMINO

Ihr holden Kleinen, sagt mir an,
Ob ich Pamina retten kann?

DIE DREI KNABEN

Dies kund zu thun, steht uns nicht an;
Sei standhaft, duldsam und
verschwiegen.
Bedenke dies; kurz, sei ein Mann,
Dann, Jüngling, wirst du männlich
siegen.

(Sie gehen ab.)

TAMINO

Die Weisheitslehre dieser Knaben
Sei ewig mir ins Herz gegraben.
Wo bin ich nun? Was wird mit mir?

PAPAGENO

Love fills all the days of our life, it is
part of nature's plan.

BOTH

Its high purpose is clear: nothing is
nobler than to be man and wife. Man
and wife together attain godliness.

CHANGE OF SCENE

(Grove, in the middle of which are three
temples. The three boys, holding silver palm
branches, enter from the left, leading Tamino,
whose flute hangs at his side.)

BOYS

This way leads to your goal. Now you
must fight bravely, remembering our
commands: be persevering, tolerant and
silent.

TAMINO

Tell me, you charming boys, if I can
save Pamina.

BOYS

It is not for us to tell you this. Be
persevering, tolerant and silent. In
short, remember to be a man, and you
will win a man's victory.

(They depart.)

TAMINO

May the wise precepts of these boys be
engraven on my heart forever. Where
am I now? What will happen? Is this

Ist dies der Sitz der Götter hier?
Es zeigen die Pforten, es zeigen die Säulen,
Dass Klugheit und Arbeit und Künste hier weilen;
Wo Tätigkeit thronet und Müssiggang weicht,
Erhält seine Herrschaft das Laster nicht leicht.
Ich wage mich mutig zur Pforte hinein,
Die Absicht ist edel und lauter und rein.
Erzitt're, feiger Bösewicht!
Pamina retten ist mir Pflicht.

STIMMEN

Zurück!

TAMINO

Zurück? So wag ich hier mein Glück!

STIMMEN

Zurück!

TAMINO

Auch hier ruft man: zurück?
Da sehe ich noch eine Tür,
Vielleicht find' ich den Eingang hier.

(Indem er sich der Mittelpforte nähert, öffnet sich diese und ein Priester tritt heraus.)

PRIESTER

Wo willst du, kühner Fremdling hin?
Was suchst du hier im Heiligtum?

TAMINO

Der Lieb' und Tugend Eigentum.

PRIESTER

Die Worte sind von hohem Sinn!
Allein wie willst du diese finden?
Dich leitet Lieb' und Tugend nicht,
Weil Tod und Rache dich entzünden.

the seat of the Gods? There are the gates, there are the pillars with 'Discretion', 'Labour' and 'Art' inscribed upon them. How can vice flourish here where industry reigns and idleness is banished? I'll dare to approach this gate. My intention is noble and pure. Tremble now, cowardly villain. My duty is to save Pamina.

VOICES

Go back.

TAMINO

Go back? Then I'll try my fortune at this door.

VOICES

Go back.

TAMINO

Here too, the call 'Go back'. Yet I see one more door. Perhaps I can enter here.

(He approaches the door, which opens. A priest comes out.)

PRIEST

Bold stranger, what do you want here? What are you seeking in this holy place?

TAMINO

I come by right of love and virtue.

PRIEST

The words are fine ones, but how will you find what you seek when it is not love and virtue that guides you, but death and revenge?

TAMINO

Nur Rache für den Bösewicht.

PRIESTER

Den wirst du wohl bei uns nicht finden.

TAMINO

Sarastro herrscht in diesen Gründen?

PRIESTER

Ja, ja! Sarastro herrschet hier!

TAMINO

(mit einigen Schritten nach links)
So ist denn alles Heuchelei!

PRIESTER

Willst du schon wieder gehn?

TAMINO

Ja, ich will gehn, froh und frei,
Nie euren Tempel sehn.

PRIESTER

Erklär' dich näher mir,
Dich täuschet ein Betrug.

TAMINO

Sarastro wohnet hier,
Das ist mir schon genug.

PRIESTER

Wenn du dein Leben liebst,
So rede, bleibe da!
Sarastro hassest du?

TAMINO

Ich hass' ihn ewig! Ja!

PRIESTER

Nur gieb mir deine Gründe an.

TAMINO

Yes, revenge upon a villain.

PRIEST

You will find no villain here.

TAMINO

Is not Sarastro your ruler?

PRIEST

True, Sarastro is our ruler.

TAMINO

(Taking a few steps to the left.)
Then all is hypocrisy here.

PRIEST

Are you going already?

TAMINO

Yes, gladly will I leave this place. I shall never enter your temple.

PRIEST

Explain yourself to me. I fear you may have been fraudulently deceived.

TAMINO

If Sarastro is ruler here, that is enough for me.

PRIEST

If your life is dear to you, speak, do not move. You hate Sarastro?

TAMINO

I shall hate him for all eternity.

PRIEST

But tell me why.

TAMINO

Er ist ein Unmensch, ein Tyrann.

PRIESTER

Ist das, was du gesagt, erwiesen?

TAMINO

Durch ein unglücklich' Weib bewiesen,
Das Gram und Jammer niederdrückt.

PRIESTER

Ein Weib hat also dich berückt?
Ein Weib tut wenig, plaudert viel.
Du, Jüngling, glaubst dem
Zungenspiel?
O legte doch Sarastro klar
Die Absicht seiner Handlung dar.

TAMINO

Die Absicht ist nur allzuklar;
Riss nicht der Räuber ohn' Erbarmen
Pamina aus der Mutter Armen?

PRIESTER

Ja, Jüngling! Was du sagst, ist wahr.

TAMINO

Wo ist sie, die er uns geraubt?
Man opferte vielleicht sie schon?

PRIESTER

Dir dies zu sagen, teurer Sohn,
Ist jetzt und mir noch nicht erlaubt.

TAMINO

Erklär' dies Rätsel, täusch' mich nicht.

PRIESTER

Die Zunge bindet Eid und Pflicht.

TAMINO

Wann also wird die Decke schwinden?

TAMINO

He is a monster, a tyrant.

PRIEST

Can you prove what you are saying?

TAMINO

It is proved by the grief of an unhappy
woman.

PRIEST

So you have been charmed by a woman.
Women do little, but talk a great deal,
and you, my boy, believe their chatter.
If only Sarastro could explain to you the
purpose of his action.

TAMINO

His purpose is only too clear. Did not
the merciless thief snatch Pamina from
her mother's arms?

PRIEST

Yes, my boy, what you say is true.

TAMINO

Where is the maiden you have stolen?
Or has she already been sacrificed?

PRIEST

I am not allowed to tell you this yet,
dear son.

TAMINO

Explain this riddle. Do not deceive me.

PRIEST

My duty and my oath forbid me.

TAMINO

When will the truth be known?

PRIESTER

Sobald dich führt der Freundschaft
Hand
Ins Heiligtum zum ew'gen Band.

(*Er wendet sich und geht langsam durch die
Mittelpforte ab.*)

TAMINO

O ewige Nacht! wann wirst du
schwinden?
Wann wird das Licht mein Auge
finden?

STIMMEN

Bald, Jüngling, oder nie!

TAMINO

Bald, sagt ihr, oder nie?
Ihr Unsichtbaren, saget mir,
Lebt denn Pamina noch?

STIMMEN

Pamina lebet noch!

TAMINO

Sie lebt? Ich danke euch dafür.
Wenn ich doch nur imstande wäre,
Allmächtige, zu eurer Ehre,
Mit jedem Tone meinen Dank
Zu schildern, wie er hier entsprang!

(*Er spielt auf seiner Flöte. Sogleich
erscheinen wilde Tiere und Vögel aller Art.
Er hört auf und sie fliehen.*)

Wie stark ist nicht dein Zauberton,
Weil holde Flöte, durch dein Spielen
Selbst wilde Tiere Freude fühlen.
Doch nur Pamina bleibt davon.
Pamina! höre, höre mich!
Umsonst! Wo? Ach, wo find' ich dich?

(*Papageno antwortet mit seinem
Faunenflötchen*)

PRIEST

As soon as friendship's hand leads you
into the temple to our everlasting
fellowship.

(*He returns to the temple.*)

TAMINO

O, eternal night, will you never end?
When shall my eyes find the light?

VOICES

Soon, or never.

TAMINO

Soon, soon, you say, or never. Tell me,
invisible ones, is Pamina still alive?

VOICES

Pamina still lives.

TAMINO

She lives? She lives? I thank you for
that. If only I knew, almighty powers,
how to offer my thanks to you for this.

(*He plays his flute. Wild animals come and
listen.*)

How gentle is your magic tone,
wondrous flute. Even the wild animals
are enchanted by it. But yet Pamina
remains a prisoner. Pamina, hear me. In
vain. Where, oh where shall I find you?

(*He hears Papageno's pipes.*)

TAMINO

Ha, das ist Papagenos Ton!
Vielleicht sah er Pamina schon,
Vielleicht eilt sie mit ihm zu mir,
Vielleicht führt mich der Ton zu ihr.

(*Er eilt hinten ab. Papageno und Pamina eilen, wenn Tamino verschwunden ist, ohne Fesseln vorn herbei*)

PAMINA UND PAPAGENO

Schnelle Füsse, rascher Mut,
Schützt vor Feindes List und Wut.
Fänden wir Tamino doch,
Sonst erwischen sie uns noch.

PAMINA

Holder Jüngling!

PAPAGENO

Stille, stille, ich kann's besser.

(*Er pfeift. Tamino antwortet hinten mit seiner Flöte*)

BEIDE

Welche Freude ist wohl grösser?
Freund Tamino hört uns schon;
Hierher kam der Flötenton.
Welch ein Glück, wenn ich ihn finde,
Nur geschwinde! nur geschwinde!

(*Monostratos tritt ihnen von dort her entgegen*)

MONOSTATOS

Nur geschwinde! nur geschwinde!
Ha, hab' ich euch noch erwischt?
Nur herbei mit Stahl und Eisen;
Wart, ich will euch Mores weisen.
Den Monostatos berücken!
Nur herbei mit Band und Stricken,
He, ihr Sklaven, kommt herbei!

(*Sklaven kommen mit Fesseln*)

TAMINO

Ah, Papageno's chimes. Perhaps he has already seen Pamina. Perhaps this sound will lead me to her.

(*He departs. Papageno and Pamina enter from another direction.*)

PAMINA AND PAPAGENO

We must hurry to escape the enemy's cunning. If only we can find Tamino, before they catch us.

PAMINA

Dearest youth!

PAPAGENO

Quiet. I can do better.

(*He plays his pipes, and the flute answers.*)

BOTH

What great joy. Tamino hears us already, that was his flute. How happy we shall be when we find him. Let us hurry.

(*They are caught by Monostatos.*)

MONOSTATOS

Yes, hurry. But now I've caught you, you will be properly chained. I'll soon teach you how to obey. You won't get around Monostatos. Come here, slaves.

(*Slaves enter with chains.*)

PAMINA, PAPAGENO

Ach, nun ist's mit uns vorbei!

PAPAGENO

Wer viel wagt, gewinnt oft viel,
Komm', du schönes Glockenspiel!
Lass' die Glöckchen klingen, klingen,
Dass die Ohren ihnen singen.

(Er spielt sein Glockenspiel.)

MONOSTATOS UND DIE SKLAVEN

(davon besänftigt, singen und tanzen nach dem Takt)

Das klinget so herrlich, das klinget so schön!
Tralla lalala trallalalala!
Nie hab' ich so etwas gehört und gesehn!
Trallalala tralla lalala!

(Sie entfernen sich singend und tanzend nach links hinten.)

PAPAGENO UND PAMINA

Könnte jeder brave Mann
Solche Glöckchen finden,
Seine Feinde würden dann
Ohne Mühe schwinden,
Und er lebte ohne sie
In der besten Harmonie.
Nur der Freundschaft Harmonie
Mildert die Beschwerden;
Ohne diese Sympathie
Ist kein Glück auf Erden!

STIMMEN

(Chor von aussen)

Es lebe Sarastro! Sarastro lebe!

PAPAGENO

Was soll das bedeuten? Ich zittre, ich bebe!

PAMINA AND PAPAGENO

Ah, now it's all over for us.

PAPAGENO

If you chance it, you often win. Come, beautiful bells, produce your magic sound.

(He plays the bells.)

MONOSTATOS AND SLAVES

(bewitched, sing and dance to the music)

What a splendid, beautiful sound.
La-la-ra-, la-la. I've never heard or seen anything like it.

(Monostatos and slaves dance off.)

PAPAGENO AND PAMINA

If only every honest man had such bells! His enemies would disappear without trouble, and men would live together in harmony without foes. Only friendship can lighten our troubles. Without such sympathy, there is no happiness on earth.

CHORUS

(within)

Hail Sarastro.

PAPAGENO

What does that mean? I'm trembling with fear.

PAMINA

O Freund, nun ist's um uns gethan!
Dies kündigt den Sarastro an.

PAPAGENO

O wär' ich eine Maus,
Wie wollt ich mich verstecken!
Wär' ich so klein wie Schnecken,
So kröch ich in mein Haus.
Mein Kind, was werden wir nun sprechen?

PAMINA

Die Wahrheit, sei sie auch Verbrechen.

(Sarastro und Gefolge treten ein.)

CHOR

Es lebe Sarastro! Sarastro soll leben!
Er ist es, dem wir uns mit Freuden
ergeben!
Stets mög' er des Lebens als Wieser sich
freun,
Er ist unser Abgott, dem alle sich weihn.

PAMINA

(kniet)

Herr, ich bin zwar Verbrecherin!
Ich wollte deiner Macht entfliehn,
Allein die Schuld ist nicht an mir—
Der böse Mohr verlangte Liebe;
Darum, o Herr! entfloh ich dir.

SARASTRO

Steh' auf, erheitere dich, o Liebe!
Denn ohne erst in dich zu dringen,
Weiss ich von deinem Herzen mehr:
Du liebst einen andern sehr.
Zur Liebe will ich dich nicht zwingen,
Doch geb' ich dir die Freiheit nicht.

PAMINA

Mich rufet ja die Kindespflicht,
Denn meine Mutter—

PAMINA

My friend, now we are really lost. It
means Sarastro has returned.

PAPAGENO

If only I were a mouse, I'd hide myself
away. Or if I were a snail, I'd creep into
my house. What on earth shall we say to
him?

PAMINA

The truth, whatever happens.

(Sarastro and priests enter.)

PRIESTS

Hail Sarastro. We praise him joyfully.
May he continue to guide us. He is as a
god, to whom we all dedicate ourselves.

PAMINA

(kneeling before Sarastro)

Lord, it is true I have committed a
crime. I meant to escape from you. But
the guilt is not all mine. I fled because
the wicked Moor molested me.

SARASTRO

Arise, dry your tears, beloved one.
Without forcing you to tell me, I know
what is in your heart. You love
someone very greatly, someone else. I
shall never compel you to love me, but
I cannot yet give you your freedom.

PAMINA

But my duty as a daughter calls to me.
My mother—

SARASTRO

Steht in meiner Macht.
Du würdest um dein Glück gebracht,
Wenn ich dich ihren Händen liesse.

PAMINA

Mir klingt der Muttername süsse;
Sie ist es—

SARASTRO

Und ein stolzes Weib.
Ein Mann muss eure Herzen leiten,
Denn ohne ihn pflegt jedes Weib
Aus seinem Wirkungskreis zu schreiten.

(Monostatos mit Tamino von links.)

MONOSTATOS

Nun, stolzer Jüngling, nur hierher,
Hier ist Sarastro, unser Herr.

PAMINA

Er ist's!

TAMINO

Sie ist's!

PAMINA

Ich glaub' es kaum!

TAMINO

Es ist kein Traum!

(Sie nähern sich beiderseitig.)

BEIDE

Es schling' mein Arm sich um sie her!
Und wenn es auch mein Ende wär'!

ALLE

Was soll das heissen?

SARASTRO

—is in my power. Misfortune would be
yours were I to place you in her hands.

PAMINA

But my mother is so dear to me. She
is—

SARASTRO

She is a proud woman. A man must
guide your heart, for, without men,
women lose the right path.

(Monostatos enters with Tamino.)

MONOSTATOS

Now proud youth, here is Sarastro, our
lord.

PAMINA

It's he.

TAMINO

It's she.

PAMINA

I can hardly believe it.

TAMINO

It's not a dream.

(They embrace.)

BOTH

Let me put my arms about you, this
may be our last moment.

ALL

What can this mean?

MONOSTATOS

Welch' eine Dreistigkeit!

(*Indem er zwischen Pamina und Tamino tritt und sie trennt.*)

Gleich auseinander, das geht zu weit!

(*Er kniet vor Sarastro.*)

Dein Sklave liegt zu deinen Füssen,
Lass den vermess'nen Frevler büssen!
Bedenk', wie frech der Knabe ist:
Durch dieses selt'nen Vogels List
Wollt' er Pamina dir entführen.
Allein ich wusst ihn auszuspüren!
Du kennst mich! Meine Wachsamkeit—

SARASTRO

Verdient, dass man ihr Lorbeer streut.
He! Gebt dem Ehrenmann sogleich—

MONOSTATOS

Schon deine Gnade macht mich reich.

SARASTRO

Nur siebenundsiebzig Sohlenstreich'

MONOSTATOS

Ach Herr, den Lohn verhofft' ich nicht!

SARASTRO

Nicht Dank', es ist ja meine Pflicht!

ALLE

Es lebe Sarastro, der göttliche Weise!
Er lohnet und strafet in ähnlichem
Kreise.

SARASTRO

Führt diese beiden Fremdlinge
In unsere Prüfungstempel ein;
Bedecket ihre Häupter dann,
Sie müssen erst gereinigt sein.

MONOSTATOS

Such boldness goes too far.

(*He separates them.*)

Separate immediately.

(*He kneels before Sarastro.*)

Your slave lies at your feet, to testify against this transgressor. See how insolent the boy is. And helped by the cunning of this rare bird here, Pamina meant to escape. But I foiled them. You know how watchful I am.

SARASTRO

You should be recompensed for your deeds. Away now to your reward—

MONOSTATOS

Your gracious words are reward enough for me.

SARASTRO

—a sound whipping.

MONOSTATOS

Oh lord, that is not what I had hoped for.

SARASTRO

Do not thank me, it is my duty.

ALL

Hail Sarastro, the godlike sage. He rewards and chastises with equal justice.

SARASTRO

Lead these two strangers into our place of trial. Cover their heads, for they must first be purified.

ALLE

Wenn Tugend und Gerechtigkeit
Den grossen Pfad mit Ruhm bestreut,
Dann ist die Erd' ein Himmelreich,
Und Sterbliche den Göttern gleich.

ALL

When justice and virtue abound on
every side, then earth will become
heaven, and mortals shall be as Gods.

ZWEITER AKT

(Unterirdischer Tempel. Die Priester treten von rechts und links ein.)

SARASTRO

Ihr, in dem Weisheitstempel
eingeweihten Diener der grossen Götter
Osiris und Isis! Mit reiner Seele erklär'
ich euch, dass unsere heutige
Versammlung eine der wichtigsten
unserer Zeit ist. Tamino, ein
Königssohn, wandelt an der nördlichen
Pforte unseres Tempels. Diesen
Tugendhaften zu bewachen, ihm
freundschaftlich die Hand zu bieten, sei
heute eine unserer wichtigsten Pflichten.
Haltet ihr ihn für würdig, so folgt
meinem Beispiel.

(Sarastro und die Priester blasen dreimal in die Hörner.)

Gerührt über die Einigkeit Eurer
Herzen, dankt Sarastro euch im Namen
der Menschheit. Man führe Tamino mit
seinem Reisegefährten im Vorhof des
Tempels ein.
Und du, Freund, vollziehe dein heiliges
Amt und lehre sie die Macht der Götter
erkennen.

ACT II

(Underground Temple. The priests assemble.)

SARASTRO

This meeting, O initiated devotees of
the great Gods Isis and Osiris, is one of
the most important of our time.
Tamino, the son of a king, waits at the
north door of our temple. In brief, he
desires to emerge from the darkness of
ignorance into the light of our holiness.
Our most important duty today is to
watch over and guard his virtuousness.
If you consider him worthy to join us,
follow my example.

(Sarastro and the priests blow a note on the horns they carry.)

In the name of mankind, I thank you
for your unanimous decision. Let
Tamino and his companion be led
within here. And you, friend,
fulfil your holy task and in your wisdom
teach them man's duty and the power of
the Gods.

SARASTRO UND PRIESTER

O Isis und Osiris, schenket
Der Weisheit Geist dem neuen Paar!
Die ihr der Wand'rer Schritte lenket,
Stärkt mit Geduld sie in Gefahr.
Lasst sie der Prüfung Früchte schon;
Doch sollten sie zu Grabe gehen,
So lohnt der Tugend kühnen Lauf,
Nehmt sie in euren Wohnsitz auf.

(Sarastro und die Priester entfernen sich in feierlicher Weise. Tamino und Papageno mit den zwei Priestern eintretten.)

ERSTER PRIESTER

Ihr Fremdlinge! was sucht oder fordert ihr von uns?

TAMINO

Freundschaft und Liebe.

ERSTER PRIESTER

Bist du bereit, es mit deinem Leben zu erkämpfen?

TAMINO

Ja.

ERSTER PRIESTER

Reiche mir deine Hand!

(Sie reichen sich die Hände.)

So!

ZWEITER PRIESTER

(zu Papageno)

Willst auch du dir Weisheitsliebe erkämpfen?

SARASTRO AND PRIESTS

O Isis and Osiris, grant wisdom to these two newcomers, lead their steps in the path of virtue, strengthen them in times of danger.
Let them be victorious in the trial, but if they should die then reward their virtue and take them to your abode.

(Sarastro and priests exit. Tamino and Papageno are led in by two priests.)

FIRST PRIEST

What has led you to this sanctuary, stranger?

TAMINO

Friendship and love.

FIRST PRIEST

And for them, would you sacrifice your life?

TAMINO

I would.

FIRST PRIEST

Give me your hand.

SECOND PRIEST

(To Papageno:)

Will you too struggle to achieve wisdom?

PAPAGENO

Kämpfen ist meine Sache nicht. Ich bin so ein Naturmensch, der sich mit Schlaf, Speis' und Trank begnügt; und wenn es ja sein könnte, dass ich nur einmal ein schönes Weibchen fange.

ZWEITER PRIESTER

Die wirst du nie erhalten, wenn du dich nicht unseren Prüfungen unterziehst.

PAPAGENO

Worin besteht diese Prüfung?

ZWEITER PRIESTER

Dich allen unseren Gesetzen zu unterwerfen, selbst den Tod nicht zu scheuen.

PAPAGENO

Ich bleibe ledig.

ZWEITER PRIESTER

Wenn nun aber Sarastro dir ein Mädchen aufbewahrt hätte, das an Farbe und Kleidung dir ganz gleich wäre?

PAPAGENO

Mir gleich? Ist sie jung?

ZWEITER PRIESTER

Jung und schön.

PAPAGENO

Und heisst?

ZWEITER PRIESTER

Papagena.

PAPAGENO

Wie?—Pa—?

PAPAGENO

I'm not very keen on struggling, and I don't really care about wisdom. I'm a natural man who's content with sleep, food and drink. If possible I'd like a beautiful wife as well.

SECOND PRIEST

These will not be yours unless you submit to our trials.

PAPAGENO

What sort of trials?

SECOND PRIEST

But if you could win a virtuous maid?

PAPAGENO

I'll stay single.

SECOND PRIEST

What if Sarastro had reserved for you a maiden just like yourself in form and feature?

PAPAGENO

Just like me? Is she young?

SECOND PRIEST

Young and beautiful.

PAPAGENO

What's she called?

SECOND PRIEST

Papagena.

PAPAGENO

What? Pa—?

ZWEITER PRIESTER

Papagena.

PAPAGENO

Papagena? Die möchte ich aus losser
Neugierde sehen.

ZWEITER PRIESTER

Sehen kannst du sie!

PAPAGENO

Aber wenn ich sie gesehen habe,
hernach muss ich sterben?
Ja?—Ich bleibe ledig.

ZWEITER PRIESTER

Sehen kannst du sie, aber bis zur
verlaufenen Zeit kein Wort mit ihr
sprechen.

ERSTER PRIESTER

(zu Tamino)

Auch dir, Prinz, legen die Götter ein
heilsames Stillschweigen auf. Du wirst
Pamina sehen, aber nicht sie sprechen
dürfen; dies ist der Anfang eurer
Prüfungszeit.

PRIESTER

Bewahret euch vor Weibertücken:
Dies ist des Bundes erste Pflicht!
Manch' weiser Mann liess sich
berücken,
Er fehlte und versah sich's nicht.
Verlassen sah er sich am Ende,
Vergolten seine Treu mit Hohn!
Vergebens rang er seine Hände,
Tod und Verzweiflung war sein Lohn.

(Beide Priester ab nach rechts.—Es wird
dunkel.)

SECOND PRIEST

Papagena.

PAPAGENO

Papagena? I'm very curious to see her.

SECOND PRIEST

You can see her.

PAPAGENO

And when I've seen her, I suppose I'll
have to die. In that case I'll stay single.

SECOND PRIEST

You can see her, but you must not
speak a word to her.

FIRST PRIEST

(To Tamino)

This same healthy silence the Gods ask
you to observe, Prince. You shall see
Pamina, but you may not speak to her.
This is the beginning of your time of
trial.

BOTH PRIESTS

Beware of woman's intriguing: this is
the first law of our band. Many a wise
man lets himself be deceived by them
without knowing it. Too late he realises
that his faith has been mocked. In vain
his regrets, his rewards then are death
and despair.

(They go out. It becomes dark.)

PAPAGENO

He! Lichter her! Lichter her!

TAMINO

Ertrag' es mit Geduld und denke, es ist
der Götter Wille.

(Die drei Damen eilen mit Fackeln)

DIE DAMEN

Wie? Wie? Wie?
Ihr an diesem Schreckensort?
Nie, nie, nie
Kommt ihr wieder glücklich fort!
Tamino, dir ist Tod geschworen!
Du, Papageno, bist verloren!

PAPAGENO

Nein, nein, nein! Das wär' zu viel.

TAMINO

Papageno, schweig still!
Willst du dein Gelübde brechen,
Nichts mit Weibern hier zu sprechen?

PAPAGENO

Du hörst ja, wir sind beide hin.

TAMINO

Stille, sag' ich! schweige still!

PAPAGENO

Immer still und immer still!

DIE DAMEN

Ganz nah' ist euch die Königin!
Sie drang im Tempel heimlich ein.

PAPAGENO

Wie? Was? Sie soll im Tempel sein?

PAPAGENO

Hey, some light here.

TAMINO

Put up with it, and remember it's the
will of the Gods.

(The three ladies enter with torches.)

LADIES

Why have you come to this dreadful
place? You will never get out alive.
Tamino, you are doomed. You,
Papageno, are lost.

PAPAGENO

No, no, that would be too much.

TAMINO

Papageno, be quiet. Do you want to
break your oath?

PAPAGENO

You heard them, we're both done for.

TAMINO

I tell you, be quiet.

PAPAGENO

Be quiet, be quiet, that's all I hear.

LADIES

Our Queen is quite close by. She has
stolen into the temple.

PAPAGENO

What's that? She's here in the temple?

TAMINO

Stille, sag' ich! schweige still!
Wirst du immer so vermessen
Deiner Eidespflicht vergessen?

DIE DAMEN

Tamino, hör'! Du bist verloren!
Gedenke an die Königin!
Man zischelt viel sich in die Ohren
Von dieser Priester falschem Sinn.

TAMINO

Ein Weiser prüft und achtet nicht,
Was der gemeine Pöbel spricht.

DIE DAMEN

Man sagt, wer ihrem Bunde schwört,
Der ist verwünscht mit Haut und Haar.

PAPAGENO

Das wär' beim Teufel unerhört!
Sag' an, Tamino, ist das wahr?

TAMINO

Geschwätz, von Weibern nachgesagt,
Von Heuchlern aber ausgedacht.

PAPAGENO

Doch sagt es auch die Königin.

TAMINO

Sie ist ein Weib, hat Weibersinn,
Sei still, mein Wort sei dir genug,
Denk' deiner Pflicht und handle klug.

DIE DAMEN

Warum bist du mit uns so spröde?
Auch Papageno schweigt—so rede!

PAPAGENO

Ich möchte gern—wohl—

TAMINO

I tell you, be quiet. Will you never stop
your impertinent chatter?

LADIES

Hear, Tamino. You are lost. Think of
our Queen. Have you not heard all that
is said about these wicked priests?

TAMINO

A wise man takes no heed of what the
vulgar mob is saying.

LADIES

They say that all who join this band are
condemned to hell.

PAPAGENO

What, go to the devil? Oh, don't let
that be true.

TAMINO

That's the tittle-tattle of hypocritical
women.

PAPAGENO

But the Queen says it.

TAMINO

She is a woman, with the senses of a
woman. Be silent. Let my word be
enough for you. Remember your duty
and be discreet.

LADIES

Why do you speak so roughly to us.
And you, Papageno, why so silent?

PAPAGENO

I would like to—

TAMINO

Still!

PAPAGENO

Ihr seht, dass ich nicht soll—

TAMINO

Still!
Dass du nicht kannst das Plaudern
lassen,
Ist wahrlich eine Schand für dich!

PAPAGENO

Dass ich nicht kann das Plaudern lassen,
Ist wahrlich eine Schand' für mich!

DIE DAMEN

Wir müssen sie mit Scham verlassen,
Es plaudert keiner sicherlich;

TAMINO, PAPAGENO

Sie müssen uns mit Scham verlassen,
Es plaudert keiner sicherlich;

ALLE

Vom festen Geiste ist ein Mann,
Er denket, was er sprechen kann.

CHOR DER PRIESTER
(von aussen)

Entweiht ist die heilige Schwelle!
Hinab mit den Weibern zur Hölle!

(Donner.)

DIE DAMEN

O weh! O weh! O weh!

(stürzen entsetzt nach links hinaus)

PAPAGENO

O weh! O weh! O weh!

(fällt vor Schrecken zu Boden)

TAMINO

Quiet.

PAPAGENO

You see, I can't—

TAMINO

Quiet! Your endless chattering is a
disgrace.

PAPAGENO

My endless chattering is a disgrace.

LADIES

In shame we must leave them, since
they won't speak to us.

TAMINO AND PAPAGENO

In shame they must leave us, since we
won't speak to them.

ALL

A man's spirit is strong: he thinks
before he speaks.

CHORUS OF PRIESTS

(off)

Our sanctuary is profaned. Away to
Hell with these women.

(Thunder)

LADIES

Help
(They disappear.)

PAPAGENO

Help, help!
(He falls to the ground.)

VERWANDLUNG

(Garten mit einem See im Hintergrund.
Pamina schlafend. Monostatos von links
hinten.)

MONOSTATOS

Alles fühlt der Liebe Freuden,
Schnäbelt, tändelt, herzt und küsst;
Und ich soll die Liebe meiden,
Weil ein Schwarzer hässlich ist!
Ist mir denn kein Herz gegeben?
Ich bin auch den Mädchen gut!
Immer ohne Weibchen leben,
Wäre wahrlich Höllenglut!
Drum so will ich, weil ich lebe,
Schnäbeln, küssen, zärtlich sein!
Lieber guter Mond, vergebe,
Eine Weisse nahm mich ein.
Weiss ist schön! ich muss sie küssen;
Mond, verstecke dich dazu!
Sollt' es dich zu sehr verdriessen,
O so mach' die Augen zu!

(Er schleicht langsam und leise zu Pamina
hin. Die Königin eilt von rechts hinten
herbei.)

KÖNIGIN

Zurück!

MONOSTATOS

O weh!

KÖNIGIN

Der Hölle Rache kocht in meinem
Herzen,
Tod und Verzweiflung flammet um
mich her!
Fühlt nicht durch dich Sarastro
Todesschmerzen,
So bist du meine Tochter
nimmermehr—
Verstossen sei auf ewig und verlassen,
Zertrümmert alle Bande der Natur,

CHANGE OF SCENE

(A garden, with a lake in the background.
Pamina is sleeping. Monostatos enters.)

MONOSTATOS

All the others know the delights of
love, kissing and flirting, but I have to
shun love because a black man is ugly
to them. But have I not a heart? Don't I
know how to handle a woman? To live
always without a wife would be
torment. So, since I'm alive, I too will
indulge in this love game. Forgive me,
moon, but I'm going to capture a white
woman. She is beautiful, I must kiss
her. Moon, hide yourself. If it's too
annoying for you, shut your eyes.

(He approaches Pamina, but there is a sound
of thunder and the Queen of the Night
appears. Pamina awakens.)

QUEEN

Keep away.

MONOSTATOS

Oh Heavens!

QUEEN

The vengeance of Hell rages in my
heart. Death and despair I intend for
him. If Sarastro does not meet his death
through you, then you are no longer my
daughter. I shall expel, forsake and
destroy forever all natural feelings if
you do not kill Sarastro. Hear, you
Gods of vengeance, hear a mother's
vow.

(Thunder. She disappears.)

Wenn nicht durch dich Sarastro wird
erblassen!
Hört! Rachegötter! Hört der Mutter
Schwur!

(Donner. Sie verschwindet.)

PAMINA

Morden soll ich? Götter! Das kann ich
nicht. Was soll ich thun?

MONOSTATOS

Dich mir anvertrauen.

PAMINA

Du weisst also?

MONOSTATOS

Alles! Du hast also nur einen Weg, dich
und deine Mutter zu retten.

PAMINA

Der wäre?

MONOSTATOS

Mich zu lieben!

PAMINA

Götter!

MONOSTATOS

Nun, Mädchen, ja oder nein!

PAMINA

Nein!

MONOSTATOS

Nein? So fahr' hin!

*(Er versucht sie zu stechen, aber Sarastro
eintritt und schleudert Monostatos zurück.)*

Herr, ich bin unschuldig!

PAMINA

Commit murder? Ye Gods, I cannot
do it. What shall I do?

MONOSTATOS

Trust in me.

PAMINA

Ah, you know then.

MONOSTATOS

Everything. So you have only one way
to save yourself and your mother.

PAMINA

And that is?

MONOSTATOS

To love me.

PAMINA

You Gods!

MONOSTATOS

Well, my girl? Yes or no?

PAMINA

No.

MONOSTATOS

No? Then die.

*(He goes to stab her, but Sarastro enters and
prevents him.)*

My lord, I am innocent.

SARASTRO

Ich weiss, dass deine Seele eben so schwarz als dein Gesicht ist. Geh!

(Er eilt nach rechts hinten ab.)

PAMINA

Herr! Strafe meine Mutter nicht!

SARASTRO

Ich weiss alles. Du sollst sehen, wie ich mich an deiner Mutter räche.
In diesen heil'gen Hallen
Kennt man die Rache nicht,
Und ist ein Mensch gefallen,
Führt Liebe ihn zur Pflicht.
Dann wandelt er an Freundes Hand
Vergnügt und froh ins bess're Land
In diesen heil'gen Mauern,
Wo Mensch den Menschen liebt,
Kann kein Verräter lauern,
Weil man dem Feind' vergiebt.
Wen solche Lehren nicht erfreun,
Verdienet nicht ein Mensch zu sein.

VERWANDLUNG

(Eine Halle. Tamino, Papageno und die zwei Priester.)

ERSTER PRIESTER

Hier seid Ihr euch Beide allein überlassen Noch einmal, vergesst das nicht: Schweigen.

ZWEITER PRIESTER

Papageno! wer an diesem Orte sein Stillschweigen bricht, den strafen die Götter durch Donner und Blitz. Leb wohl!

SARASTRO

I know all too much already, I know that your soul is as black as your face. Go.

PAMINA

Lord, do not punish my mother.

SARASTRO

I know everything. I know that she prowls about in the underground chambers of the temple, brooding on revenge against me and all mankind. But you shall see how I avenge myself on her. Heaven only grant the noble youth courage and steadfastness in his holy task, then you shall be happy with him, and your mother in shame shall retreat to her castle. In this holy place, we do not know vengeance. If a man strays, love guides him back to his duty. Then, led by friendship's hand, he travels cheerfully to a better land. Within these holy walls, men love one another. And if a traitor should be found, he is forgiven. He who cannot find joy in these teachings is not worthy to be called a man.

CHANGE OF SCENE

(A Hall, Tamino, Papageno and the two Priests.)

FIRST PRIEST

Here you shall both be left alone. Once again, do not forget: be silent.

SECOND PRIEST

Papageno! Thunder and lightning from the Gods strike whoever breaks his silence in this place. Farewell.

PAPAGENO

Das ist ein lustiges Leben! Wär ich lieber im Walde, so hört ich doch manchmal einen Vogel pfeifen.

TAMINO

St!

PAPAGENO

Mit mir selbst werd' ich wohl sprechen dürfen.

TAMINO

St!

PAPAGENO

La la la! Nicht einmal einen Tropfen Wasser bei kommt man bei diesen Leuten, viel weniger sonst was. (*Ein altes Weib tritt ein.*) Ist das für mich?

WEIB

Ja, mein Engel.

PAPAGENO

Nicht mehr und nicht weniger als Wasser. Geb her, Alte, setze dich zu mir, mir währt die Zeit verdammt lange. Sag' mir, wie alt bist du?

WEIB

Achtzehn Jahr und zwei Minuten.

PAPAGENO

Achtzehn Jahr und zwei Minuten! Hast du auch einen Geliebten?

WEIB

Freilich.

PAPAGENO

It's a merry life. I wish I were back in the forest where you still hear a bird singing sometimes.

TAMINO

Shh!

PAPAGENO

Surely I'm allowed to talk to myself?

TAMINO

Shh!

PAPAGENO

Shh yourself. These people don't even give you a drop of water, let alone anything else.

(*An old woman enters, and offers him water.*)

Is that for me?

WOMAN

Yes, my angel.

PAPAGENO

Just as I thought, it's only water. Come here, old woman, come and sit by me, it's so boring here. Tell me, how old are you?

WOMAN

Eighteen years and two minutes.

PAPAGENO

Eighteen years and two minutes! And have you a lover?

WOMAN

Of course.

PAPAGENO

Ist er auch so jung wie du?

WEIB

Er ist um zehn Jahr älter.

PAPAGENO

Wie nennt sich denn dein Liebhaber?

WEIB

Papageno.

PAPAGENO

Papageno! Sag' mir, wie heisset du
denn!

WEIB

Ich heisse—

PAPAGENO

O weh! Nun sprech' ich kein Wort
mehr.

*(Die drei Knaben kommen von links; der
eine trägt die Flöte, der andere das
Glockenspiel.)*

KNABEN

Seid uns zum zweitenmal willkommen,
Ihr Männer in Sarastros Reich.
Er schickt, was man euch abgenommen,
Die Flöte und die Glöckchen euch.
Wollt ihr die Speisen nicht
verschmähen,
So esset, trinket froh davon.
Wenn wir zum drittenmal uns sehen,
Ist Freude eures Mutes Lohn!
Tamino, Mut!
nah' ist das Ziel.
Du, Papageno, schweige still!

(Sie gehen weg.)

PAPAGENO

Is he as young as that, too?

WOMAN

He's about ten years older.

PAPAGENO

What's this lover's name?

WOMAN

Papageno.

PAPAGENO

Papageno? Tell me then, what's your
name?

WOMAN

I'm called—

PAPAGENO

Help! I shan't say another word.

*(The three boys enter, bringing a table spread
with food, as well as the flute and the
chimes.)*

BOYS

A second time we greet you in
Sarastro's kingdom. He returns to you
the flute and the bells. If this food is not
too lowly for you, eat and drink of it.
When we see you for the third time, joy
shall be the reward of your courage. Be
brave, Tamino, the goal is near. You,
Papageno, keep silent.

(They depart.)

PAPAGENO

Tamino! wollen wir nicht speisen?

(Tamino bläst auf seiner Flöte)

Blase du nur fort auf deiner Flöte, ich
will meine Brocken blasen. Herr
Sarastro führt eine gute Küche. Nun,
ich will sehen, ob auch der Keller so gut
bestellt ist. Ha, das ist Götterwein!

(Pamina eilt herbei.)

PAMINA

Du hier? Gütige Götter! Dank euch!
Aber du bist traurig? Sprichst nicht eine
Silbe mit deiner Pamina? Papageno,
sage du mir, was ist meinem Freund?
Wie? Auch du? O das ist mehr als Tod!
Ach, ich fühl's, es ist verschwunden,
Ewig hin der Liebe Glück!
Nimmer kommt ihr, Wonnestunden,
Meinem Herzen mehr zurück!
Sieh' Tamino, diese Thränen,
Fliessen, Trauter, dir allein.
Fühlst du nicht der Liebe Sehnen,
So wird Ruh' im Tode sein!

(Sie geht)

VERWANDLUNG

(Ein Zimmer in dem Tempel)

SARASTRO UND PRIESTER

O Isis und Osiris, welche Wonne.
Die düstre Nacht verscheucht der Glanz
der Sonne.
Bald fühlt der edle Jüngling neues
Leben;
Bald ist er unserm Dienste ganz
ergeben.
Sein Geist ist kühn, sein Herz ist rein,
Bald wird er unser würdig sein.

PAPAGENO

Tamino, why not let's eat?

(Tamino plays the flute.)

Blow away at your flute then, and I'll
blow this lovely food away. Lord
Sarastro keeps a good kitchen. Let's see
if his cellar is equally good. Hm, this
wine is fit for the Gods.

(Pamina enters.)

PAMINA

You here? I thank the Gods for leading
me this way. But you are sad? Have
you not one word for your Pamina?
What, you want me to go? Do you no
longer love me?
I am to flee from you without knowing
why? Papageno, tell me, what is the
matter with him?
Oh, this is worse than illness, worse
than death. My only beloved. Ah, I feel
that the happiness of love has departed
from me forever. You hours of rapture,
my heart will never know you again.
See, Tamino, these tears are flowing for
you alone. If you no longer love me, I
can find repose only in death.

(She goes.)

CHANGE OF SCENE

(A room in the temple.)

SARASTRO AND PRIESTS

O Isis and Osiris, how wondrous it is to
know that gloomy night is being
dispelled by the sun's light. Soon the
noble youth will feel new life within
him, soon he will enter into our
communion. His spirit is daring, his
heart pure, soon he will be worthy.

SARASTRO

Prinz! Dein Betragen war bis hierher
männlich und gelassen. Deine Hand!
Man bringe Pamina!

*(Zwei Priester entfernen sich nach links vorn
und kommen sogleich mit Pamina zurück.)*

PAMINA

Wo bin ich? Sagt, wo ist mein
Jüngling?

SARASTRO

Hier.

PAMINA

Tamino!

TAMINO

Zurück!

PAMINA

Soll ich dich, Teurer, nicht mehr sehn?

SARASTRO

Ihr werdet froh euch wieder sehn.

PAMINA

Dein warten tödliche Gefahren!

TAMINO

Die Götter mögen mich bewahren!

SARASTRO

Die Götter mögen ihn bewahren!

PAMINA

Du wirst dem Tode nicht entgehen;
Mir flüstert dieses Ahnung ein.

SARASTRO

Prince, your bearing so far has been
manly and composed. Give me your
hand. Bring in Pamina.

(Pamina is brought in.)

PAMINA

Where am I? Tell me, where is my
beloved?

SARASTRO

He is here.

PAMINA

Tamino!

TAMINO

Away from me!

PAMINA

Shall I never see you again, my dearest?

SARASTRO

They will meet again, joyfully.

PAMINA

The most fearsome dangers await you.

TAMINO

The Gods will keep me safe.

SARASTRO

The Gods will keep him safe.

PAMINA

I cannot rid myself of the fear that you
will die.

SARASTRO

Der Götter Wille mag geschehen,
Ihr Wink soll ihm Gesetze sein.

TAMINO

Der Götter Wille mag geschehen,
Ihr Wink soll mir Gesetze sein!

PAMINA

O liebtest du, wie ich dich liebe,
Du würdest nicht so ruhig sein.

TAMINO

Glaub' mir, ich fühle gleiche Triebe,
Werd' ewig dein Getreuer sein!

SARASTRO

Glaub' mir, er fühlet gleiche Triebe,
Werd' ewig dein Getreuer sein!
Die Stunde schlägt, nun müsst ihr scheiden!

TAMINO UND PAMINA

Wie bitter sind der Trennung Leiden!

SARASTRO

Tamino muss nun wieder fort.

TAMINO

Pamina, ich muss wirklich fort!

PAMINA

Tamino muss nun wirklich fort!

SARASTRO

Nun muss er fort!

TAMINO

Nun muss ich fort!

PAMINA

So musst du fort!

SARASTRO

Whatever the Gods may will, their
word shall be his law.

TAMINO

Whatever the Gods may will, their
word shall be my law.

PAMINA

If you loved me as I do you, you would
not be so calm.

TAMINO

Believe me, I feel the same emotion, and
shall be always faithful to you.

SARASTRO

Believe me, he feels the same emotion,
and will be always faithful to you. The
hour has struck. Now you must part.

PAMINA AND TAMINO

How bitter are the sorrows of parting.

SARASTRO

Now Tamino must go.

TAMINO

Pamina, now I must go.

PAMINA

Tamino, must you really go?

SARASTRO

Now he must go.

TAMINO

Now I must go.

PAMINA

Then you must go.

TAMINO

Pamina, lebe wohl!

PAMINA

Tamino, lebe wohl!

SARASTRO

Nun eile fort.
Dich ruft dein Wort.
Die Stunde schlägt, wir sehn uns wieder!

TAMINO UND PAMINA

Ach, goldne Ruhe, kehre wieder!

PAPAGENO

Tamino! Tamino! Wenn ich nur
wenigstens wüsste, wo ich wäre?

STIMME

Zurück!

PAPAGENO

Barmherzige Götter! Wo wend' ich
mich hin? Wenn ich nur wüsste, wo ich
hereinkam.

STIMME

Zurück!

PAPAGENO

Nun kann ich weder zurück noch
vorwärts, muss vielleicht am Ende gar
verhungern! Schon recht! Warum bin
ich mitgereist!

(Der erste Priester tritt vor.)

ERSTER PRIESTER

Mensch! du hattest verdient, auf immer
in finstern Klüften der Erde zu wandern;
die gütigen Götter aber erlassen dir die
Strafe—Dafür wirst du das himmlische
Vergnügen der Eingeweihten nie fühlen.

138

TAMINO

Pamina! Farewell!

PAMINA

Farewell, Tamino.

SARASTRO

Now hasten away. Your word calls you.
The hour has struck, we shall meet
again.

TAMINO AND PAMINA

Ah, blissful peace, return to us.

PAPAGENO

Tamino, Tamino! If only I knew where
I was!

A VOICE

Keep away.

PAPAGENO

Merciful Gods, if only I knew which
way I came in.

A VOICE

Keep away.

PAPAGENO

Now I can't go back or forwards. Am I
to die here of hunger? It's my own
fault, why did I agree to come?

(First priest enters.)

FIRST PRIEST

Fellow, you deserve only to wander for
ever in the bowels of the earth, yet the
kindly Gods will not punish you. The
heavenly joys of the brotherhood,
however, you will never know.

PAPAGENO

Mir wäre jetzt ein gutes Glas Wein das grösste Vergnügen.

PRIESTER

Sonst hast du keinen Wunsch in dieser Welt?

PAPAGENO

Bis jetzt nicht.

ERSTER PRIESTER

Man wird dich damit bedienen.

(Er geht. Sofort kommt ein Becher aus der Erde.)

PAPAGENO

Juhe! Da ist er schon!

(Er trinkt.)

Herrlich!—Himmlisch!—Göttlich!
Ha! Mir wird ganz wunderlich ums
Herz; ich möchte—ich wünschte—ja,
was denn?
Ein Mädchen oder Weibchen
Wünscht Papageno sich.
O so ein sanftes Täubchen
Wär' Seligkeit für mich!
Dann schmeckte mir Trinken und
Essen,
Dann könnt ich mit Fürsten mich
messen,
Des Lebens als Weiser mich freu'n,
Und wie im Elysium sein.
Ein Mädchen oder Weibchen
Wünscht Papageno sich.
O, so ein sanftes Täubchen
Wär' Seligkeit für mich.
Ach, kann ich denn keiner von allen
Den reizenden Mädchen gefallen?
Helf' eine mir nur aus der Not,

PAPAGENO

The most heavenly joy to me just now would be a glass of good wine.

FIRST PRIEST

Apart from that, is there nothing else in the world you desire?

PAPAGENO

Not at the moment.

FIRST PRIEST

Then you shall have your desire.

(He goes. A glass of wine magically appears.)

PAPAGENO

Hurray, it's here already. Splendid.

(He drinks)

Heavenly! Fit for the Gods! Oh, my heart feels so strange. I want to—I'd like—what would I like? A girl or a wife is what Papageno wants. A gentle little dove would be absolute bliss. I'd eat and drink and be as happy as a prince. It would be like being in Elysium. Can't I have just one of all the charming girls in the world? If not one of them will come and ease my distress, then I shall really pine away and die. If no one will love me, then flames of hell will consume me. But one kiss from a woman and I'd be healthy again.

Sonst gräm' ich mich wahrlich zu Tod.
Ein Mädchen oder Weibchen
Wünscht Papageno sich.
O, so ein sanftes Täubchen
Wär' Seligkeit für mich.
Wird keine mir Liebe gewähren,
So muss mich die Flamme verzehren!
Doch küsst mich ein weiblicher Mund,
So bin ich schon wieder gesund!

(Die alte Dame tritt vor.)

WEIB

Da bin ich schon, mein Engel.

PAPAGENO

Du hast dich meiner erbarmt?

WEIB

Ja, mein Engel.

PAPAGENO

Das ist ein Glück.

WEIB

Und wenn du mir versprichst, mir ewig
treu zu bleiben, so sollst du sehn, wie
zärtlich dich dein Weibchen lieben
wird; komme, reich' mir deine Hand.

PAPAGENO

Nur nicht so hastig, liebes Kind.

WEIB

Papageno; ich rathe dir, zaudre nicht.
Deine Hand, oder du bist auf immer
hier eingekerkert.

PAPAGENO

Eingekerkert? Nein, da will ich doch
lieber eine Alte nehmen, als gar keine—
Nun, da hast du meine Hand, mit der

(The old woman enters.)

OLD WOMAN

I'm right here, my angel.

PAPAGENO

You feel sorry for me?

OLD WOMAN

Yes, my angel.

PAPAGENO

What luck!

OLD WOMAN

And if you promise to be faithful to me
forever, you will see how tenderly your
little wife will love you. Come, give me
your hand.

PAPAGENO

Don't be so hasty, dearest.

OLD WOMAN

Papageno, I advise you not to hesitate.
Give me your hand or you will be
imprisoned here forever.

PAPAGENO

Imprisoned? Well, I'd rather take an old
woman than none at all. There, you
have my hand, and you can be sure that

Versicherung, dass ich dir immer getreu
bleibe so lang ich keine schönere sehe.

WEIB

Das schwörst du?

PAPAGENO

Ja das schwör ich dir.

*(Da fällt die Verkleidung ab, und es
erscheint ein Junges Mädchen)*

Pa—Pa—Papagena!

ERSTER PRIESTER

Fort von hier! er ist deiner noch nicht
würdig.

VERWANDLUNG

(Kurzer Palmengarten.)

DIE DREI KNABEN

Bald prangt, den Morgen zu verkünden,
Die Sonn, auf gold'ner Bahn!
Bald soll der Aberglaube schwinden,
Bald siegt der weise Mann.
O holde Ruhe, steig' hernieder,
Kehr' in der Menschen Herzen wieder;
Dann wird die Erd' ein Himmelreich,
Und Sterbliche den Göttern gleich.

ERSTER KNABE

Doch seht, Verzweiflung quält
Paminen.

ZWEITER UND DRITTER KNABE

Wo ist sie denn?

ERSTER KNABE

Sie ist von Sinnen.

I'll always be true—so long as I don't
see anything prettier.

OLD WOMAN

You swear that?

PAPAGENO

Yes, I swear it to you.

(The old woman turns into a young girl.)

Pa-Pa-Paganena!

FIRST PRIEST

Away from here. He is not yet worthy
of you.

CHANGE OF SCENE

(A garden of palms.)

BOYS

Soon the golden sun will rise to greet
the morning. Soon superstition will
disappear, and wisdom will triumph.
Oh golden repose, come down into the
hearts of men again. Then will earth
become heaven, and mankind one with
the Gods.

FIRST BOY

But look, Pamina is in despair.

SECOND AND THIRD BOYS

Where is she?

FIRST BOY

Her senses are deranged.

DIE DREI KNABEN

Sie quält verschmähter Liebe Leiden.
Lasst uns der Armen Trost bereiten!
Füwahr, ihr Schicksal geht mir nah!
O wäre nur ihr Jüngling da!—
Sie kommt, lasst uns beiseite gehn,
Damit wir, was sie mache, sehn.

PAMINA

(zu dem Dolch)

Du also bist mein Bräutigam?
Durch dich vollend' ich meinen Gram!

DIE KNABEN

Welch' dunkle Worte sprach sie da?
Die Arme ist dem Wahnsinn nah'.

PAMINA

Geduld, mein Trauter, ich bin dein,
Bald werden wir vermählet sein.

DIE KNABEN

Wahnsinn tobt ihr im Gehirne;
Selbstmord steht ihr auf der Stirne.
Holdes Mädchen, sieh uns an!

PAMINA

Sterben will ich, weil der Mann,
Denn ich nimmermehr kann hassen,
Seine Traute kann verlassen.
Dies gab meine Mutter mir.

DIE KNABEN

Selbstmord strafet Gott an dir.

PAMINA

Lieber durch dies Eisen sterben,
Als durch Liebesgram verderben.
Mutter, durch dich leide ich,
Und dein Fluch verfolget mich.

BOYS

She suffers from unrequited love, let us try to comfort her. Her plight grieves us. If only her beloved were here. Here she comes, let us go to her so that we can see what she means to do.

PAMINA

(holding a dagger)

You then shall be my bridegroom. Through you, I'll end my torments.

BOYS

What fearful words she utters. The poor woman is close to madness.

PAMINA

Be patient, beloved, I am yours. Soon we shall be wedded.

BOYS

Her mind is disordered. She intends to kill herself. Dear maiden, look on us.

PAMINA

I shall die, since the man whom I could never hate has forsaken me. My mother gave me this knife.

BOYS

God will punish suicide.

PAMINA

I would rather die by this knife than pine away in hopeless love. Mother, mother, my sorrows come from you, and your curse follows me.

DIE KNABEN

Mädchen, willst du mit uns gehn?

PAMINA

Ha, des Jammers Mass ist voll!
Falscher Jüngling, lebe wohl!
Sieh, Pamina stirbt durch dich:
Dieses Eisen töte mich.

(Sie will sich erstechen. Die Knaben
entreissen ihr den Dolch)

DIE KNABEN

Ha, Unglückliche! halt ein!
Sollte dies dein Jüngling sehen,
Würde er vor Gram vergehen;
Denn er liebet dich allein.

PAMINA

Was? Er fühlte Gegenliebe?
Und verbarg mir seine Triebe,
Wandte sein Gesicht von mir?
Warum sprach er nicht mit mir?

DIE KNABEN

Dieses müssen wir verschweigen,
Doch, wir wollen dir ihn zeigen!
Und du wirst mit Staunen sehn,
Dass er dir sein Herz geweiht,
Und den Tod für dich nicht scheut.

PAMINA

Führt mich hin, ich möcht' ihn sehen

DIE KNABEN

Kommt, wir wollen zu ihm gehen.

ALLE VIER

Zwei Herzen, die von Liebe brennen,
Kann Menschenohnmacht niemals
trennen.
Verloren ist der Feinde Müh',
Die Götter selbst beschützen sie.

BOYS

Maiden, will you go with us?

PAMINA

Ah, my misery could not be greater.
False youth, farewell. See, Pamina dies
for you. Let this knife kill me.

(She tries to stab herself, but the boys prevent
her.)

BOYS

Stop, unhappy maid. If your lover
could see this, he would disperse your
sorrows, for he loves you alone.

PAMINA

What? He loves me, yet hides, turns his
face from me? Why did he not speak to
me?

BOYS

This we may not tell you, yet we can
take you to him. You will be astonished
to see that his heart is yours, and that he
will even face death for you. Come, let
us go to him.

PAMINA

Lead me there. I must see him.

BOYS

Come, we will go to him.

ALL

Man has no power to separate two
hearts that burn with love. The enemy
is powerless, for the Gods themselves
protect them.

VERWANDLUNG

(Der Tempel)

DIE GEHARNISCHTEN

Der, welcher wandert diese Strasse voll
Beschwerden,
Wird rein durch Feuer, Wasser, Luft
und Erden;
Wenn er des Todes Schrecken
überwinden kann,
Schwingt er sich aus der Erde
himmelan.
Erleuchtet wird er dann imstande sein,
Sich den Mysterien der Isis ganz zu
weihn.

TAMINO

Mich schreckt kein Tod, als Mann zu
handeln,
Den Weg der Tugend fortzuwandeln.
Schliesst mir die Schreckenspforten auf,
Ich wage froh den kühnen Lauf.

PAMINA

(von draussen)

Tamino, halt! Ich muss dich sehen.

TAMINO

Was hör' ich? Paminens Stimme?

DIE GEHARNISCHTEN

Ja, ja, das ist Paminens Stimme.

TAMINO UND DIE GEHARNISCHTEN

Wohl mir, nun kann sie mit mir gehn,
Nun trennet uns kein Schicksal mehr,
Wenn auch der Tod beschieden wär'!

TAMINO

Ist mir erlaubt, mit ihr zu sprechen?

CHANGE OF SCENE

(The temple.)

ARMED MEN

The man who, full of troubles, treads
this path will be purified by fire, water,
air, and earth. If he can overcome the
fear of death, he will rise to glorious
heights. Then, enlightened, he will
know the mysteries of Isis.

TAMINO

Death has no terrors for me. Let me
tread the path to virtue. Open the
dreadful gates. Gladly I'll dare to know
what lies beyond.

PAMINA

(outside)

Tamino, wait. I must see you.

TAMINO

What do I hear? Pamina's voice?

ARMED MEN

Yes, that is Pamina's voice.

TAMINO AND ARMED MEN

Thank Heaven, she can come with me.
Now no fate can part us,
not even death itself.

TAMINO

Am I allowed to speak to her?

DIE GEHARNISCHTEN

Dir sei erlaubt, mit ihr zu sprechen!

TAMINO UND DIE GEHARNISCHTEN

Welch' Glück, wenn wir euch
wiedersehn.
Froh Hand in Hand im Tempel gehn.
Ein Weib, das Nacht und Tod nicht
scheut,
Ist würdig und wird eingeweiht.

*(Die beiden Priester kommen mit Pamina
von rechts.)*

PAMINA

Tamino mein! o welch' ein Glück!

TAMINO

Pamina mein! o welch' ein Glück!
Hier sind die Schreckenspforten,
Die Not und Tod mir dräun.

PAMINA

Ich werd' an allen Orten
An deiner Seite sein.
Ich selber führe dich,
Die Liebe leite mich.
Sie mag den Weg mit Rosen streun,
Weil Rosen stets bei Dornen sein.
Spiel du die Zauberflöte an,
Sie schütze uns auf unsrer Bahn.
Es schnitt in einer Zauberstunde
Mein Vater sie aus tiefstem Grunde
Der tausendjähr'gen Eiche aus,
Bei Blitz und Donner, Sturm und
Braus.
Nun komm' und spiel' die Flöte an,
Sie leite uns auf grauser Bahn.

PAMINA, TAMINO UND DIE
GEHARNISCHTEN

Wir wandeln durch des Tones Macht,
Froh durch des Todes düst're Nacht!

ARMED MEN

You are allowed to speak to her.

TAMINO AND ARMED MEN

What joy to meet again and go joyfully
hand in hand into the temple. A woman
who has no fear of night and death is
worthy to be one of us.

(Pamina is brought in.)

PAMINA

My Tamino. Oh, what happiness.

TAMINO

My Pamina. Oh, what happiness.
Here are the gates of terror, beyond
which pain and death lie in wait for me.

PAMINA

Wherever you go, I shall stay by your
side. I myself will lead you as love
guides me. Love's roses along the way
shall cover the thorns. Play the magic
flute: it will protect us on our journey.
In a time of enchantment during
thunder, lightning, and raging storm,
my father carved it from the bough of a
thousand-year-old oak. Come, play it, it
will lead us on our dangerous way.

PAMINA, TAMINO AND ARMED MEN

Joyfully we journey through death's
gloomy night, by the magic of its
sound.

(*Tamino und Pamina wenden sich nach links zur Feuerhöhle, die sie durchwandern, und kommen wieder heraus.*)

TAMINO UND PAMINA

Wir wandelten durch Feuergluten,
Bekämpften mutig die Gefahr.
Dein Ton sei Schutz in Wasserfluten,
So wie er es im Feuer war.

(*Tamino und Pamina wenden sich nun ganz wie vorhin nach rechts zur Wasserhöhle. Sobald sie aus der Wasserprobe herauskommen: Die Vorigen. Sarastro, die Priester hoch oben im Tempel.*)

Ihr Götter! Welch' ein Augenblick!
Gewähret ist uns Isis Glück.

PRIESTER

Triumph! Triumph! du edles Paar!
Besieget hast du die Gefahr,
Der Isis Weihe ist nun dein,
Kommt, tretet in den Tempel ein!

VERWANDLUNG

(*Kurze Gartendekoration; Papageno allein, mit einem Strick umgürtet.*)

PAPAGENO

Papagena! Papagena! Papagena!
Weibchen! Täubchen! Meine Schöne!
Vergebens! Ach, sie ist verloren!
Ich bin zum Unglück schon geboren.
Ich plauderte—und das war schlecht,
Darum geschieht es mir schon recht.
Seit ich gekostet diesen Wein,
Seit ich das schöne Weibchen sah,
So brennt's im Herzenskämmerlein,
So zwickt es hier, so zwickt es da.
Papagena! Herzenstäubchen!
Papagena! liebes Weibchen!
's ist umsonst! Es ist vergebens!

(*Tamino and Pamina go off into a hall of fire. He plays the flute. They return.*)

TAMINO AND PAMINA

We journeyed through the flames, braving all dangers. Now let your sound protect us from water as it protected us from fire.

(*They go off this time through another door, walking through water. Tamino plays the flute again. They return. The gates of the temple are thrown open, revealing Sarastro and the priests waiting to welcome them.*)

You Gods, what a sight. The bliss of Isis descends on us.

PRIESTS

Triumph, O noble pair. You have braved the dangers, and are now consecrated to Isis. Come, enter the temple.

CHANGE OF SCENE

(*A garden. Papageno enters carrying a rope.*)

PAPAGENO

Papagena, Papagena. My little wife, my little dove, my pretty one. No use, she is lost. I was born to be miserable. I chattered away all the time. That was awful, and it serves me right. Since I tasted that wine and saw that beautiful creature, my heart's been on fire and I don't know where I am. Papagena, my heart's darling. Papagena, my dear little dove! Ah, it's no use. I'm tired of life now: death will put an end to the love that burned within me. I'll hang myself from this tree, since life has no more pleasure for me. Farewell, wicked world. Since you misuse me so and deny me a beloved mate, it's all over. I

146

Müde bin ich meines Lebens!
Sterben macht der Lieb' ein End',
Wenn's im Herzen noch so brennt.
Diesen Baum da will ich zieren,
Mir an ihm den Hals zuschnüren,
Weil das Leben mir missfällt;
Gute Nacht, du falsche Welt.
Weil du böse an mir handelst,
Mir kein schönes Kind zubandelst:
So ist's aus, so sterbe ich,
Schöne Mädchen, denkt an mich.
Will sich eine um mich Armen,
Eh' ich hänge, noch erbarmen,
Wohl, so lass ich's diesmal sein!
Rufet nur, ja—oder nein.—
Keine hört mich, alles stille!
Also ist es euer Wille?
Papageno, frisch hinauf!
Ende deinen Lebenslauf.
Nun, ich warte noch, es sei,
Bis man zählet, eins, zwei, drei.
Eins! Zwei! Drei!
Nun wohlan, es bleibt dabei!
Weil mich nichts zurücke hält!
Gute Nacht, du falsche Welt.

*(Er will sich aufhängen. Die drei Knaben
eilen von links herbei.)*

DIE KNABEN

Halt ein, o Papageno, und sei klug;
Man lebt nur einmal, dies sei dir genug.

PAPAGENO

Ihr habt gut reden, habt gut scherzen.
Doch brennt es euch, wie mich im Herzen,
Ihr würdet auch nach Mädchen gehn.

DIE KNABEN

So lasse deine Glöckchen klingen,
Dies wird dein Mädchen zu dir bringen.

PAPAGENO

Ich Narr vergass der Zauberdinge!
Erklinge, Glockenspiel, erklinge!

shall die. Beautiful maiden, remember me. But if someone will have pity on me before I kill myself, then I might put it off this time. Just say yes or no. No one hears me, everything is silent. Do you all want me to die? All right, Papageno, put an end to life's misery. No, I'll wait for a moment. I'll count one, two, three. One! two! . . . three! Well then, that's settled. Nothing can hold me back now. Farewell, false world.

(He is about to hang himself when the three boys enter.)

BOYS

Stop! Papageno, be clever. You have only one life, so don't waste it.

PAPAGENO

It's all very well for you to talk and joke, but if your hearts were on fire like mine, you'd be pining for girls too.

BOYS

Play your bells. They will bring your wife to you.

PAPAGENO

What a fool I am, I forgot that magical toy. Tinkle, bells, I must see my dear sweetheart.

Ich muss mein liebes Mädchen sehn.
Klinget, Glöckchen, klinget,
Schafft mein Mädchen her!
Klinget, Glöckchen, klinget,
Bringt mein Weibchen her!

(Die drei Knaben eilen unter diesem Schlagen nach links ab und kehren sogleich mit Papagena zurück)

DIE KNABEN

Nun, Papageno, sieh' dich um!

(Sie entfernen sich nach links.)

PAPAGENO

Papagena!

PAPAGENA

Papageno!

PAPAGENO

Bist du mir nun ganz gegeben?

PAPAGENA

Nun bin ich dir ganz gegeben.

PAPAGENO

Nun, so sei mein liebes Weibchen!

PAPAGENA

Nun, so sei mein Herzenstäubchen!

BEIDE

Welche Freude wird das sein!
Wenn die Götter uns bedenken,
Uns'rer Liebe Kinder schenken,
So liebe kleine Kinderlein!

PAPAGENO

Erst einen kleinen Papageno!

PAPAGENA

Dann eine kleine Papagena!

148

Tinkle, little bells, bring my sweetheart here, bring me my little wife.

(The boys return with Papagena.)

BOYS

Now, Papageno, look at her.

(The boys depart.)

PAPAGENO

Papagena!

PAPAGENA

Papageno!

PAPAGENO

Are you now completely mine?

PAPAGENA

Yes, now I am completely yours.

PAPAGENO

You shall be my dear wife.

PAPAGENA

You shall be my beloved little dove.

BOTH

What joy it will be if the Gods allow our love to be blessed with children, lovely little children.

PAPAGENO

First a little Papageno.

PAPAGENA

Then a little Papagena.

PAPAGENO

Dann wieder einen Papageno!

PAPAGENA

Dann wieder eine Papagena!

BEIDE

Papagena! Papagena! Papagena!
Es ist das höchste der Gefühle,
Wenn viele, viele, viele, viele
Pa—Pa—Pa—Pa—geno,
Pa—Pa—Pa—Pa—gena,
Der Segen froher Eltern sein.

VERWANDLUNG

(Der Tempel—Es ist Nacht. Monostatos,
Die Königin mit ihren Drei Damen.)

MONOSTATOS

Nur stille! stille! stille!
Bald dringen wir im Tempel ein.

KÖNIGIN UND ALLE DAMEN

Nur stille! stille! stille! stille!
Bald dringen wir im Tempel ein.

MONOSTATOS

Doch Fürstin, halte Wort! Erfülle—
Dein Kind muss meine Gattin sein.

KÖNIGIN

Ich halte Wort; es ist mein Wille.

ALLE DAMEN

Ihr Kind soll deine Gattin sein.

MONOSTATOS

Doch still! ich höre schrecklich
Rauschen,
Wie Donnerton und Wasserfall.

PAPAGENO

Then another Papageno.

PAPAGENA

Then another Papagena.

BOTH

Papagena! Papagena! Papagena!
What a glorious feeling it will be to
have so many, many, children.
Pa-Pa-Pa-Pa-geno,
Pa-Pa-Pa-Pa-gena,
The blessing of happy parents.

CHANGE OF SCENE

(In front of the temple. Night. Monostatos
enters with the Queen and the three ladies.)

MONOSTATOS

Quietly now, soon we shall be in the
temple.

QUEEN AND LADIES

Quietly now, soon we shall be in the
temple.

MONOSTATOS

But, great sovereign, you must keep
your word. Your child must become my
wife.

QUEEN

I shall keep my word. It is my will that
my child shall be your wife.

LADIES

Her child shall become his wife.

MONOSTATOS

But, quiet. I hear a terrible rumbling
like thunder or rushing water.

KÖNIGIN UND DAMEN

Ja, fürchterlich ist dieses Rauschen,
Wie fernen Donners Wiederhall.

MONOSTATOS

Nun sind sie in des Tempels Hallen.

ALLE

Dort wollen wir sie überfallen—
Die Frömmler tilgen von der Erd'
Mit Feuersglut und mächt'gem Schwert.

MONOSTATOS UND DIE DAMEN

Dir grosse Königin der Nacht,
Sei unsrer Rache Opfer gebracht.

(Sie versinken.—Man hört starken Donner, Sturm.)

ALLE

Zerschmettert, vernichtet ist unsere Macht,
Wir alle gestürzet in ewige Nacht.

(Sonnentempel. Priester und Priesterinnen. Sarastro steht erhöht. Vor ihm Tamino und Pamina, beide in priesterlicher Kleidung. Die Priester auf beiden Seiten. Die drei Knaben halten Blumen.)

SARASTRO

Die Strahlen der Sonne vertreiben die Nacht,
Zernichten der Heuchler erschlichene Macht.

CHOR DER PRIESTER

Heil sei euch Geweihten! Ihr dranget durch Nacht,
Dank sei dir, Osiris und Isis, gebracht!
Es siegte die Stärke und krönet zum Lohn—
Die Schönheit und Weisheit mit ewiger Kron!

QUEEN AND LADIES

Yes, how frightening is this sound of distant thunder.

MONOSTATOS

Now they are all in the temple.

ALL

There we shall take them by surprise,
and sweep the sanctimonious hypocrites
away with fire and sword.

MONOSTATOS AND LADIES

To you, great Queen of the Night, we
dedicate ourselves.

(They disappear. There is a sound of thunder.)

ALL

Our power is shattered. We are all
condemned to endless night.

(A great light floods the temple. The gates open to reveal Sarastro and the priests, the boys, Tamino and Pamina.)

SARASTRO

The sun's rays drive away night and
destroy the power of the hypocrites.

PRIESTS

Hail, you dedicated ones. You have
emerged from night. Thanks to Isis and
Osiris. They fought bravely and are
rewarded with eternal beauty and
wisdom.

Chronology
Major Compositions
Further Reading

Chronology

1756   Mozart was born on January 27 at No 225 (now No 9) Getreidegasse in Salzburg. His father Leopold had served the Archbishops of Salzburg as violinist and, from 1757, as court composer. A few months after Wolfgang's birth he published an important treatise on violin technique which brought him further repute and reasonable financial reward. He married Anna Maria Pertle in 1747 when he was 28 and she was 27. Three children were born in successive years but each one died. In July, 1751, a daughter Maria Anna (always known as Nannerl) was born and survived. Two further children died soon after birth before Wolfgang was born to become the only other survivor out of seven. By the age of three Mozart was making his first attempts to play an instrument and the following year his father started giving him lessons. By the age of five he had begun to compose short pieces, and his father was beginning to understand that his son had exceptional genius and decided to train him to be a famous musician. Nannerl also had a lesser musical talent.

1762   Leopold took his children on a tour of Austria, Bavaria and Hungary. Mozart amazed everyone with his playing and was frequently asked to demonstrate various tricks of memory and his ability to improvise. In Vienna he played before the Empress and her family.

1763   After six months at home in Salzburg the entire family set out on a three and a half year tour of Europe, taking in München, Augsburg, the Rhine, Aix-la-Chapelle, Brussels, Paris, Versaille and thence to London where they stayed for a year and Mozart came under the influence of Johann Christian Bach. They came back through Holland, Paris, Dijon, Lyons, Switzerland and Bavaria. Both children had serious illnesses before they arrived back in Salzburg in 1766.

1767   Wrote his first stage work *Apollo et Hyacinthus* which was performed at Salzburg University. By this time he had written some early symphonies and keyboard concertos and numerous sonatas.

1768   Commissioned to write an opera for Vienna, *La finta semplice*, but owing to jealous intrigues the performance did not take place, and it was later produced in Salzburg. Also wrote the *singspiel, Bastien und Bastienne*. Second tour of Austria with Vienna as a base.

1769   Mozart and his father set out on an Italian tour which lasted till 1771 and took them as far as Naples. At Milan he was commissioned to write an opera to open the next season, *Mitridate, Re di Ponto*, which he eventually conducted himself from the keyboard and which proved a great triumph. There were concerts in Florence, Rome and Naples and the Pope awarded Mozart the Order of the Golden Spur.

1771   Back in Salzburg for a while, but further commissions and concerts soon took them back to Italy. Wrote the Oratorio *La Betulia liberata*.

1772   Wrote a dramatic serande *Il sogno de Scipione* for the new Prince-Archbishop Colloredo, who now became his employer. Wrote numerous symphonies and serenades for court use and many items of church music. Wrote the opera *Lucio Silla* for performance in Milan.

1774   Wrote *La finta giardiniera* for performance in Munich.

1776   Growing discontent at the dictatorial terms of employment under Colleredo, but a continual flow of musical compositions included the *Haffner* serenade and a number of fine masses.

1777   Set out for a visit to Paris with his mother with many concerts on the way. Tried but failed to get employment in Münich. In Mannheim fell in love with Aloysia Weber and intended to accompany her family on a visit to Italy, but was ordered by his father to continue on the proposed trip to Paris. It turned out to be a fruitless and tragic visit, except for a commissioned ballet *Les Petits Riens*. His mother was taken ill and died in Paris on July 3. He stayed for a while with the Weber family in Munich but the love affair cooled off and he returned to Salzburg, where he continued in his old employment.

1781   A commission from Munich led to the first of his great operas *Idomeneo*. Went to Vienna with the Archbishop of Salzburg where his increasing frustration at his servant status led to an angry resignation and dismissal.

1782   Mozart settled in Vienna, lodging with the Weber family, and eventually married Aloysia's younger sister Constanze in St Stephen's Cathedral on August 4, immediately after the triumphant production of his opera *Die Entführung aus dem Serail (Il Seraglio)*. He managed to take on a few pupils but failed to get a Court appointment in Vienna.

1783   During the next few years in Vienna composed some of his finest Piano Concertos and six quartets dedicated to Haydn whom he had first met in 1781.

1784   Became a Freemason in Vienna.

1786   His greatest operatic triumph in collaboration with Lorenzo Da Ponte was *The Marriage of Figaro* first produced on May 1. It had tremendous success in Vienna and Prague and led to new commissions.

1787   *Don Giovanni* premièred in Prague was an even greater success than *Figaro*. Leopold Mozart died in May. Mozart, in spite of his operatic successes still found it hard to make a living and began a humiliating period of having to borrow from his fellow Masons.

1788   In a depressed state but still managed to write his three last great symphonies, Nos 39, 40 and 41, in the space of a few weeks. *Don Giovanni* was produced without success in Vienna and Mozart's financial situation became worse. Although he was appointed Court Composer to the Emperor the salary was a meagre one.

1789   Visited Berlin and was offered the post of Kapellmeister but felt that he could not leave Vienna.

1790   The poverty and distress continued and matters were made more difficult by his wife's ill-health. A third opera with Da Ponte—*Così fan tutte*—staged in Vienna in January. Declined the offer of a tour in England where Da Ponte had now established himself.

1791   Wrote *The Magic Flute* for Schikaneder's theatre and *La Clemenza di Tito* for a coronation festivity in Prague. Mozart, now ill and thoroughly despondent, was visited by a mysterious stranger who asked him to write a Requiem mass for a rich and eccentric nobleman. Mozart saw it as a portent of his own end. He died, with the Requiem unfinished, on December 5. After the funeral service at St Stephen's, which Constanze was too ill to attend, he was buried in an unmarked grave in the churchyard of St Mark's.

Major Compositions

(The dates in brackets are those of composition)

Operas

Bastien und Bastienne, K50 (1768)
La finta semplice, K51 (1768)
Mitridate, Rè di Ponto, K87 (1770)
Lucio Silla, K135 (1772)
La finta giardiniera, K196 (1774/5)
Il Rè pastore, K208 (1775)
Zaide, K344 (1779)
Idomeneo, Rè di Creta, K366 (1780/1)
Die Entführung aus dem Serail, K384 (1781/2)
Der Schauspieldirektor, K486 (1786)
Le Nozze di Figaro, K492 (1786)
Don Giovanni, K527 (1787)
Così fan tutte, K588 (1790)
Die Zauberflöte, K620 (1791)
La Clemenza di Tito, K621 (1791)

Choral

La Betulia liberata K115 (1771)
Mass No 4, K139 (1771–2)
Mass No 6 (*Missa brevis*), K192 (1774)
Mass No 7, K194 (1774)
Litaniae Lauretanae, K195 (1774)
Litaniae de venerabili altaris sacremento, K243 (1776)
Mass No 10 (*Spatzenmesse*), K258 (1776)
Mass No 13 (*Orgel solo*), K275 (1777)
Mass No 14 (*Krönungs-Messe*), K317 (1779)
Mass No 16 (*Grosse Messe*), K427 (1782/3)
Motet: *Ave verum corpus*, K618 (1791)
Mass No 19 (Requiem), K626 (1791)

Symphonies

Symphony No 27 in G, K199 (1773)
Symphony No 28 in C, K200 (1773)
Symphony No 29 in A, K201 (1774)
Symphony No 32 (Overture), K318 (1779)
Symphony No 35 in D (*Haffner*), K385 (1782)
Symphony No 36 in C (*Linz*), K425 (1783)
Symphony No 38 in D (*Prague*), K504 (1786)
Symphony No 39 in E-flat, K543 (1788)
Symphony No 40 in G-minor, K550 (1788)
Symphony No 41 in C (*Jupiter*), K551 (1788)

Serenades

Serenade No 6 in D (*Serenata notturna*) K239 (1776)
Serenade No 7 in D (*Haffner*) K250 (1776)
Serenade No 8 in D (*Notturno For Four Orchestras*), K286 (1776/7)
Serenade No 9 in D (*Posthorn*), K320 (1779)
Serenade No 10 in B-flat (*Thirteen Wind Instruments*), K361 (1781)
Serenade No 13 in G (*Eine kleine Nachtmusik*), K525 (1787)

Concertos

Piano Concerto No 5 in D, K175 (1773)
Concertone in C, K190 (1773)
Bassoon Concerto in B-flat, K191 (1774)
Violin Concerto No 1 in B-flat, K207 (1775)
Violin Concerto No 2 in D, K211 (1775)
Violin Concerto No 3 in G, K216 (1775)
Violin Concerto No 4 in D, K218 (1775)
Violin Concerto No 5 in A, K219 (1775)
Piano Concerto No 6 in B-flat, K238 (1776)
Piano Concerto No 7 (2-pianos) in F, K242 (1776)
Piano Concerto No 8 in C, K246 (1776)
Violin Concerto No 6 in E-flat, K268 (1780)
Piano Concerto No 9 in E-flat, K271 (1777)
Violin Concerto No 7 in D, K271a (1777)
Flute and Harp Concerto in C, K299 (1778)
Flute Concerto in G, K313 (1778)

Flute Concerto in D (or Oboe), K314 (1778)
Sinfonia concertante in E-flat, K364 (1779)
Piano Concerto No 10 in E-flat (3-pianos), K365 (1779)
Horn Concerto No 1 in D, K412 (1782)
Piano Concerto No 11 in F, K413 (1782/3)
Piano Concerto No 12 in A, K414 (1782)
Piano Concerto No 13 in C, K415 (1782/3)
Horn Concerto No 2 in E-flat, K417 (1783)
Horn Concerto No 3 in E-flat, K447 (1783)
Piano Concerto No 14 in E-flat, K449 (1784)
Piano Concerto No 15 in B-flat, K450 (1784)
Piano Concerto No 16 in D, K451 (1784)
Piano Concerto No 17 in G, K453 (1784)
Piano Concerto No 18 in B-flat, K456 (1784)
Piano Concerto No 19 in F, K459 (1784)
Piano Concerto No 20 in D-minor, K466 (1785)
Piano Concerto No 21 in C, K467 (1785)
Piano Concerto No 22 in E-flat, K482 (1785)
Piano Concerto No 23 in A, K488 (1786)
Piano Concerto No 24 in C minor, K491 (1786)
Horn Concerto No 4 in E-flat, K495 (1786)
Piano Concerto No 25 in C, K503 (1786)
Piano Concerto No 26 in D 'Coronation', K537 (1788)
Piano Concerto No 27 in B-flat, K595 (1791)
Clarinet Concerto in A, K622 (1791)

Chamber Music
Clarinet Quintet in A, K581 (1789)

Further Reading

(General)

Anderson, Emily (ed): *The Letters of Mozart and his Family*, 2 vols (Macmillan, London 1966)

Blom, Eric: *Mozart* (Dent 'The Master Musicians Series', London, 1935; revised 1962; reprinted 1974)

Deutsch, Otto Erich: *Mozart: a Documentary Biography* (Black, London, 1965)

Einstein, Alfred: *Mozart: His Character, His Work* (Cassell, London, 1946; 2nd ed. 1956; reprinted 1978)

Hutchings, Arthur: *Mozart: The Man, The Musician* (Thames & Hudson, London, 1976)

Landon, H. C. Robbins and Mitchell, Donald (eds): *The Mozart Companion* (Rockliff, London, 1956) [incl. 'The Operas' by Gerald Abraham]

(Operas and The Magic Flute)

Batley, E. M.: *A Preface to 'The Magic Flute'* (Dobson, London 1969)

Chailley, Jacques: *The Magic Flute, Masonic Opera* (Laffont, Paris, 1966; Gollancz, London, 1972)

Dent, Edward J.: *Mozart's Operas* (Oxford University Press, London, 1913; revised 1947)

Hughes, Spike: *Famous Mozart Operas* (Hale, London, 1957)

Liebner, Janos: *Mozart on the Stage* (Calder & Boyars, London, 1972)

Mann, William: *The Operas of Mozart* (Cassell, London, 1977)

Newman, Ernest: *Opera Nights* (Putnam, London, 1943)

Osborne, Charles: *The Complete Operas of Mozart: A Critical Guide* (Gollancz, London, 1978)

(Reference)

Köchel, Ludwig Ritter von: *Der Kleine Köchel* (Breitkopf & Hartel, Leipzig, 1951); *Mozart Verzeichnis* (1937 and reprints; etc)

Acknowledgments

The illustrations are reproduced by kind permission of the following: Archiv für Kunst und Geschichte, Berlin: 14, 17, 19, 22, 53, 73, 76, 77; Archives Snark/Bibliothèque de l'opéra: 23, 58; Vienna State Opera: 61; British Library (Ray Gardner): 37, 42, 47, 49, 78; Clive Barda: 69; Covent Garden Archive (Angelo Hornak): 20, 92; Decca Record Company Limited: 93, 94; EMI Limited: 93 (Godfrey Macdomnic), 95, 96 (Photo Gérard Neuvecelle); Glyndebourne Festival Opera: 66 (Guy Gravett), 91; Hagen-Bilderdienst, Salzburg: 83; Houston Rogers: 56, 64, 68, 97; Mary Evans Picture Library: 63, 82; Metropolitan Opera Archives: 20, 74, 80 (Louis Mélançon), 44, 79; Mozarteum, Salzburg: 12, 17, 28, 29, 33, 43, 88; Opera Magazine: 66, 83, 84, 91; Pressebüro der Salzburger Festspiele: 70; Radio Times Hulton Picture Library: 11, 30, 38, 55, 60; Raymond Mander and Joe Mitchenson Theatre Collection: 91; Southern Television: 6; Teatro Comunale, Florence: 84.